Sailaday OK

Recovery from addictions through
marine-based adventure psychotherapy

Richard Lannowe Hall BEM

Cover image by: Oliver Parrish. Monkey Puzzle, Cornwall
Book design by: SWATT Books Ltd

Printed in the United Kingdom
First Printing, 2021

ISBN: 978-1-8384607-0-9 (Paperback)
ISBN: 978-1-8384607-1-6 (eBook)

Richard Lannowe Hall BEM
Churchtown, Cornwall TR16 4QZ

Praise for *"Sailaday OK"*

"This book is an inspiring story of the author's personal narrative of overcoming addiction, and his professional journey of helping others heal. Through his own experiences with trauma and addiction recovery, the author embarks on a personal and professional journey that leads to the creation and implementation of a therapeutic sailing program that incorporates marine-based adventure therapy. The book provides the story of how this program developed and the impact it had on participants' self-concept, resilience, and self-esteem. In reading the story of the authors' personal evolution, and the concurrent evolution of this innovative adventure therapy program, one cannot help but be buoyed by a sense of optimism and hope that outdoor experiential therapy may offer respite from the often intractable pain of addiction. Blending personal narratives, theory and research, this book will be useful for both clients and practitioners looking for options beyond talk therapy and the medical model of addictions treatment."

Dr. Christine Lynn Norton, LCSW, CCAT, CCTP, CET
Professor, Texas State University School of Social Work
Research Scientist, Outdoor Behavioral Healthcare Center

"there is no wi fi in the forest but you find a better connection"
    One thing that aids recovery from addiction is connection - with others and with nature.
    This book by Richard Hall about what motivated him to start up the ground breaking adventure therapy charity Sailaday OK and what was achieved as a result, is informative, inspiring, poignant and funny all at the same time.
    Sailing is unpredictable. Sometimes the waters are calm, and at other times they are turbulent. Participants learn that if you get caught in a vortex you must stay perfectly still. For an addict this is no easy task.

Countless people have found the experience of sailing with Richard life-changing. This book is a fitting tribute to what was achieved by assisting troubled people find a deep connection with themselves and others through the power of nature.

Alison Cameron MA FRSA
Director
Alison Cameron Consulting, Health & Social Care

Table of Contents

Foreword

RICHARD HALL AND I met at a Psychology of Vision, Abundance Workshop in 1998. We shared a common interest in personal development and psychotherapy; I was recovering from co-dependency and he was recovering from substance and alcohol addiction. We fell in love and set about having the first Adult-Adult, interdependent, rather than co-dependent (enmeshed with the other) or counter-dependent (avoiding the other), relationship in our lives.

As we familiarised ourselves with this strange new, healthier relational environment, I was witness to the many benefits that Richard gained for his own recovery through being aboard a boat and through sailing. Indeed, He introduced me to sailing and I spent many enriching and healing hours there myself, lazing and adventuring with him.

Very few individuals recover from substance and alcohol addiction, so Richard's personal and professional stories are very inspiring, and in my opinion, there is much important learning to be gleaned from them. My vivid memories of that time include how very seriously he took his recovery, how disciplined he was in paying attention to his physical, emotional and spiritual wellbeing during this time and how being in nature, at sea seemed to magnify the positive impact of his efforts to heal.

We both understood the importance of the natural environment as our ultimate container in the world, it's positive or negative impact on how we feel about ourselves, others and the world. At that time, neither of us had heard of, let alone studied, polyvagal theory and the autonomic nervous system, but we intuitively knew that our organisms were intimately supported or undermined by the environments we placed ourselves in; and not just the physical environments but also the relational environments, our relationships with others and the internal relationship with ourselves.

Richard skilfully took all these variables and synthesised them into the unique maritime based adventure therapy that he presents here. He would situate participants in a good physical environment and also a good psychological environment using the therapeutic relationship to create emotional safety and security; this optimal environment enabled participants firstly to settle themselves and then to stretch. In this milieu, where trauma symptoms were normalised and feelings of shame were reduced, Richard facilitated as good a relationship as he could with participants, facilitated as good a relationship as he could between participants and lastly, facilitated participants to have as good a relationship as they could with their self.

In my experience, the most effective therapy models and methodology emerge out of firstly, personal experience and secondly, professional experience. Richard drained every last drop of goodness out of his own recovery process and began sharing it with others; his Transactional Analysis psychotherapy training, his helping experience, the feedback from participants and referrers and engaging in supervision, have all contributed to the emergence of an evidence based, highly effective and easily transferrable psychotherapeutic intervention for marine based adventure therapy.

His therapy model, an ingenious blend of Transactional Analysis Psychotherapy and Adventure Therapy, is revealed organically across the pages. At the heart of Transactional Analysis psychotherapy, and at the heart of Richard's work, is the strengthening of the Adult ego state; that is the most grown up, present in the here and now part of us, able to contain intense emotion and not act out or flee from it, put language to experience, reflect and problem solve and express thoughts and feelings and get needs met in a straight way.

The development of a better functioning Adult ego state involves healing difficult Child experiences, growing up parts of us that got left behind and transforming unhelpful, usually negative, Parent messages, all of which can keep us trapped in the past and operating well below our potential. The activity of sailing, together with Richard's therapeutic facilitation, invited participants to consolidate and enhance the Adult resources they had already developed and to develop new Adult resources. Childhood injuries could be healed, and unhelpful parent communications replaced, through experiencing the kind of reparative helping relationship that Richard was skilled at offering.

This book is a delight to read. I love that each chapter is headed with a nautical term followed by an explanation. A multitude of metaphors are used intentionally to support the therapeutic process, my favourite one being, alchemy as a metaphor for change, 'where raw base metals are subjected to great heat and turned into gold'. The language in the book powerfully evokes the atmosphere of the marine environment, of the day- to-day experience of being on board a boat, the relationship dynamics, and all the human triumphs and struggles that being at sea, being in recovery, being in relationship and being in therapy deliver.

Richard's model of understanding addiction and methodology are in contrast to mainstream interventions. His therapy model doesn't focus exclusively on the management of symptoms in general, or of cravings in particular, but from the outset, addresses the underlying cause. It's rare to find an addict or other trauma survivor who hasn't experienced some kind of abuse or neglect in their early life; people who were well nurtured in their early life don't reach for substances or alcohol when they're in pain, they reach for people. The matrix of relationships fostered on board have consistently enabled participants to feel their discomfort, to feel their pain, not to flee from it but to share it with others and process it.

In conclusion, it's my opinion, Richard has made an outstanding contribution to the addiction and psychotherapy field for which he rightly received a British Empire Medal, richly deserved. I'm very proud to have been associated with Richard and his ground-breaking, Sailaday OK programme. In his book he shares with us the great variety of positive wellbeing outcomes that participants would identify in their feedback; what he doesn't mention though, and what I would like to note here is that, on a few occasions, quite some time after a participant had completed one, two or three sessions, Richard would receive a postcard or an email thanking him again for all his help and telling him that their experience with him had literally saved their life.

Finally, I paraphrase a fitting quote that I heard recently, the gist of which was, 'an encounter with nature consistently gives more than is sought'; well, Sailaday OK participants would regularly say that the programme had exceeded their expectations, it had given them much more than they had sought. I hope the text in this book will give you more than you had sought, it certainly did that for me.

Sue Parker Hall Psychotherapy Services Ltd
Certified transactional analyst (psychotherapy); MSc (Counselling & Supervision) MBACP (senior accredited practitioner); EMDR practitioner

1

Keep an Even Keel

Keep an even keel: In rough seas, Jack proves that he can balance his heart and his head, but it's sometimes tough for Jack to maintain his steely exterior and keep an even keel.

I WOKE UP to a very wet and windy morning on the boat *Physis*.[1] She was tied up on the pontoon at Falmouth, and I had sailed in the evening before from Helford as there was a gale coming. The boat was rocking, the rigging was rattling, and the rain was drumming on the decking. A whole range of noises competed with each other, creating violent and chaotic symphonies. I was hoping to sleep on for another hour before getting up and preparing the boat for the four participants shortly to be arriving for the next Sailaday OK session. This was due to be four days and nights of residential marine adventure therapy; 'due to be' being the operative phrase as the weather looked pretty gruesome.

So many chores to do – cleaning, tidying, preparing bedding, and I was also going to have to find a gap in the rain to get to Tesco to buy fresh food, bread and milk. The group were expected at midday and I was worried that they were going to be soaked through by the time they had walked from the train station. I had a phone link to one of them and sent a text suggesting that they should grab a taxi.

So, over a cup of tea and a cooked breakfast I studied their intake notes. These gave me a very brief insight into their social and medical history, their

---

1   Physis: the name given to the boat. First used by pro socratic Greek philosophers. In its first use it has a connection to nature and is the first creative power. In TA, transactional analysis, we understand the term is the energy that we connect with to help us develop onwards and upwards, a positive metaphysical energy.

present condition and a little about their wants and needs. I had prepared evaluation reports to be filled in partly on arrival and to be completed when they dispersed four days later. However, I wanted to be clear in my head about what each of them was contracting to, what they might want from the next four days. It was important for me to be absolutely clear about the needs of each individual and then to assess the group's goals, their ambitions and expectations. I definitely did not want to end up being just the ferryman, ferrying them about having a nice time on the boat – Sailaday OK was capable of offering so much more.

It was June 2011, and the participants were our first 'returnees'[2] mentoring group, people (in this case, four women) who had come out on the boat before with me, when they had been in residential addiction centres. Now they were back living in the community and this programme was designed to support them as they experienced and tackled the very real problems they faced maintaining their recovery, and finding their place back out in the world, hopefully becoming positive members of the community. The problems they might face are very real, especially around re-establishing relationships with family, possibly children and partners, as well as all the difficulties in starting again a new life looking for new jobs or training and managing money. These groups I called our RATs, our Returnee Adventure Therapees.

As the weather forecasts for the next 24 hours sounded pretty dreadful, my anxiety increased, not just about their safety but how I was going to manage four participants when we might not be able to do much in the way of sailing. How on earth was this going to be beneficial? Were we just going to sit around on the boat all day with nothing to do? They are going to get bored, frustrated and possibly angry. Oh dear, I could feel myself getting highly anxious. This was not the image I wanted to project – I felt far from the calm professional skipper and psychotherapist.

By midday the wind was screeching in the masts and stays, the noise becoming quite extreme, as there were 20 or more other boats all around me, banging against the pontoons and rattling loose rigging. When tied to a pontoon in weather like this the motion of the boat is jarring, there is no rhythm to it. It's uncomfortable, unpredictable and can feel unsafe; I was concerned that this might traumatise my already vulnerable clients.

The participants met up at Falmouth Town railway station, and arrived at Falmouth Haven pontoon together by taxi, having taken my advice. My morning tasks were done, and the boat looked ready even if I wasn't. I made

---

2 Returnees: my descriptive name for participants who have been out with Sailaday OK previously.

them welcome and we settled down in the main cabin with hot drinks, after temporarily stashing their bags and belongings around the boat.

This was always an important moment in establishing trust and relationships. These first transactions were vital in giving me an indication as to the condition of the individuals. I needed to tune into the signals of their body language and the words they used. The weather was a suitable subject for us to play the game 'Ain't it awful'. Here we could find common ground and bond, and I was pleasantly surprised to find that most of them were pretty accepting even if they were not completely aware of some of the implications.

The next part of the programme was to reintroduce them to *Physis* and familiarise them with the boat, the internal living and sleeping arrangements, and where they would each like to sleep. Also remind them about the operation of the toilet and the cooker and the limitations around electricity and water. Just generally making sure that they would feel at home and at ease.

This orientation was shortly followed by my little pep talk to re-state their reasons for being there – a therapeutic session to help them in their journey of recovery individually and as a group. Using sailing as a vehicle, as a means to explore their relationship with the external natural world, with the other members of the group and, most importantly, how they relate internally and increase their personal awareness. Awareness of their feelings and their thinking, helping them to make the tweaks necessary for them to be more efficient and more successful in their recovery and their lives.

I would remind them of why I use sailing in this way: I would point out to them that from the very moment they stepped on to the pontoon and on to the boat their world had changed. Everything was mobile for a start, nothing was quite as it was a few hours ago, they were in an ever-changing environment, and they needed to increase their levels of here and now awareness and adapt. To be more present, more aware of just being, of their being. The environment is changing moment to moment, visually and physically, and that's even before we start sailing. I would remind them that we will also use other exercises to help them increase their sense of being, using disciplines such as meditation and Tai Chi, but also to be very aware of how they express themselves. I would encourage them to express themselves verbally, to say how they were thinking, feeling, being. I would remind them that it is no good telling me they've had "a f****ing great day", as that doesn't really mean very much to me. However, when they tell me they've "had a f***ing great day because when they were doing (a) they began to feel (b)", then I begin to get an idea of why they had a great day. When speaking and using words there is a part of themselves that will be listening to what they say, their higher consciousness. It's like having an internal communication with the part of themselves that has probably been asleep for quite some time and is now only just waking up. This is an important part of the process of increasing self-awareness and consequently resilience.[3]

Returning to my preparation work for this therapy session, a simple lunch of soup, bread, cheese, cold meats and cake was the ideal environment for each participant to verbalise an oral contract, with me and the group, discussed and written down by me in front of everybody so that we all knew what each one wanted to achieve, giving me clarity about how I can help, but including each member of the crew as a participant in the process.

During this process it became abundantly clear that all four of them, in the previous weeks or months, had experienced quite a lot of trauma in their lives. For one of them it had been a devastating but short-lived relapse, and amongst the others there had been fights with family, loss of living accommodation due to lack of money, and the loss of a parent. There had been accidents and health issues. These were all highly significant events in their lives, and for people who were just finding their feet back in the world these were major stumbling blocks. I therefore found it remarkable and encouraging that they'd still managed to make the trip down to Falmouth and had committed to this programme. I was also encouraged by the changes that they had managed to make in the months since I'd last met them; physically they seemed to have grown up. They were each more present, more communicative and, even though they seemed tired and exhibiting some degrees of stress and anxiety, they were also cheerful and full of humour. I was aware of my anxiety and excitement, as all four were in quite a vulnerable place, a good jumping-off point to make long-lasting changes, but I was fearful that the weather conditions would exasperate these vulnerable and willing people and cause more traumas, or, even worse, the Sailaday OK experience might become traumatic.

During lunch I explained that it was not safe to go sailing that day and was expecting some rather negative reaction to this. However, much to my surprise, they expressed some relief, and after further discussion I realised that they were exhausted and just happy to be here on the boat with good mates around them. They felt secure and relatively safe, and quite happy to do very little. A siesta with no time limit was voted for. They each knew how to make themselves hot drinks, sandwiches and help themselves to cold drinks and biscuits or anything else they needed. We were still plugged into

---

3   Resilience: individuals' ability to adapt in the face of adverse conditions. I understand resilience to be developed and will give the person greater ability to bear the unbearable.

electricity on the pontoon so we could use a fan heater and be warm, dry and comfortable. They said they liked listening to the wildness outside, as it increased their sense of intimacy and cosiness. I went to my cabin in the stern and we all had an extended siesta.

I'd worked with one of these participants twice before, when she was in a residential centre. When she came out the second time with the residential groups, she took on a leadership role, as I liked to take one person from previous sessions to come on the next one, not just to act as a guide and leader to others in the group, but also to be a buffer between myself and the group, helping me and increasing the person's self-confidence and skills.

I had a reasonable idea of the issues facing this group of returnees. They all included some form of abuse either very early in their lives or more recently. They had all suffered trauma, not just as part of the consequence of being abused but also in their addiction careers. Drinking or using drugs to the point of becoming unconscious is a traumatic event for the body, and the lifestyle and relationships in which they find themselves in order to maintain their addictions, can cause multiple traumas. Two of these had suffered abuse from their fathers and I am always very aware of the delicate relationship I have with them and that I need to keep very clear boundaries. For them to have a positive experience when in close proximity and sharing such an intimate space in a boat with a male, there have to be clear boundaries and good communications. Many participants have voiced the fact that having a safe and trusting relationship with a male has been a profound and positive life-changing experience for them.

We came together later in the day and discussed our options, what might happen during the rest of that day and the following days. I explained and passed on any information I had about weather and tried to clarify what was safe and not safe. Although one of them was very keen to go out that afternoon and "*have an exciting time*", as she definitely had a hankering for a bit of high adrenaline sailing, I explained the safety aspects and decided against it. However, we did negotiate that they could have some time to walk around the town together if they liked, as long as they stayed together and came back at a set time. Two of them took up this option and the remaining two were quite happy to stay on the boat, reading and talking with me. We had a further look at the weather situation and decided that if it did slacken as was predicted we could set off after breakfast the following morning.

At 5:00pm we came back together again as a group in time for them to cook our supper. I had bought the provisions and their job was to put it together as a meal. It was fairly simple – chicken curry, rice, hot drinks and cake. This event was also a therapeutic task, as they needed to negotiate who was chef and who were the helpers – many a good meal has been ruined by too many cooks!

After dinner, as with all groups, we had a formal one-hour group therapy session. I tend to avoid the phrase 'therapy session' and prefer to call it a process group. This becomes a time to reflect on what is happening for them right now, how today has been, and how they have managed. It is quite likely that the day might well have served as a catalyst to bring up thoughts and feelings from the past and this would be a good time to process them and other issues that might be hampering them in their lives, together with opportunities and events that they wanted to expand on and hence enhance their lives.

What was interesting about this day was how each of them had reacted positively to this rather enforced quiet time and lack of activity. They had all arrived looking forward to the sailing and had wanted to get out there and do lots of doing, even though they were quite frightened of going out in conditions that were beyond their capability. They now realised that what each of them was really in need of doing was very little, just spending some time processing the last few days' or weeks' trauma and finding some sort of peace and safety with like-minded people. This was something I could not possibly have arranged or planned for; the rough weather had turned out to be a godsend. It was exactly what was needed. Here we were, sitting in our own peaceful little world, sorting out our various difficulties, while the outside world seemed to be going mad, ranting, raving and storming.

I learnt a lot from this process and I also gained a clear indication of where each of these participants were in their recovery. How strong was this recovery, how adaptable and how able were they to manage change? The essence of recovery is change; the ability to change and to manage change. To do this one needs to increase one's resilience and self-awareness. This is something that will crop up again and will be discussed in greater detail later in the book. But these four women certainly had enough resilience to adapt to what could have been an extremely difficult day.

The other change I noticed, to varying degrees of success in each of the crew, was their ability not to drop into the familiar role of being a victim. In active addiction and early recovery, a recurring way of seeing oneself and managing the stresses of the world around you is to adopt the position of victim. Following on from this, there can then be a tendency for some to move from the role of victim to that of perpetrator, if only to keep the drama going. However it plays out, they then blame the other or others for their behaviour. However, on this day, with this group, none of that happened. They could have blamed the bad weather, or me, Cornwall or anything else that would have helped them in their discomfort. However, that day on the boat they embraced an opportunity and let go of their expectations of how the day was going to be and consequently benefited in many ways by embracing this day of inaction and passivity. They remained vulnerable, vocal and communicative, willing to share how they were feeling. This filled me with hope for the next few days and I felt optimistic that I had four people who were well grounded in their recovery.

This was a great lesson for me – learning to work with nature. I can't control the weather, I can only work with it, and trust that it is always for the best. All my best efforts of planning the first 24 hours of that session had been thwarted. I could not have foretold what was really needed by all five of us; yet we were being offered exactly what was needed. So here in action, and quite beyond my control, is the essence of adventure therapy. Making this connection with nature and tuning in and adapting to what we have been given and making this work for us, to help us in our growth. This is not something you can learn from a textbook; this is about experiential education: "It is likely that one cannot understand a thing until we have experienced it inwardly." (Jung, psychologist)[4] Experiential educationalists believe that when you're in the 'here and now' this is the optimum state to be in for changes to take place. Relational analysts believe that experience is the foundation for internal change.

This process is so counter to our cultural and Western way of thinking about nature. When it's in the way we remove it; we can take and abuse it for our own gratification. The more isolated that humans become from the natural world, the more difficult it becomes for them to grasp or understand the struggle with which we are now engaged. This causes anxiety, frustration and a sense of being overwhelmed, which results in abnormal or irrational behaviour and a desire to reconcile the internal conflict. What once was a self-identity derived from a deep and profound relationship with the natural world is now shaped by a highly industrialised, technological and geopolitical world driven by consumption. As Paul Wachtel wrote,[5] "The idea of more, of ever-increasing wealth, has become the centre of our identity, and our security, and we are caught by it as the addict is caught by his drugs." Eco psychologists and authors like Shepard

---

4   (1) Jung CG, 1971, *Psychological Types*, London, Routledge & Kegan Paul, *Collected Works of C.G. Jung*, Vol. 6.; Jung *Analytical Psychology and the Bible* "It is a well-known fact that we cannot know a thing until we have experienced it" (1953-1978)

5   As Paul Wachtel (1989, p. 71) wrote, "The idea of more, of ever-increasing wealth, has become the centre of our identity, and our security, and we are caught by it as the addict is caught by his drugs."

(1982)[6] believe that, as people struggle as individuals to define themselves in a technological and consumer-driven world, an inner voice from which people evolved tells them to respect their place in the beautiful, powerful, and mysterious processes of the natural world. The voice begs people to change their habit of consumption and the way they live, providing hundreds of examples of the social, economic, and environmental effects of this dysfunctional behaviour. The groups I worked with clearly had been affected by primarily chemical addictions but there is an underlying issue of disconnection from our inner nature and from our outer nature that is not just confined to drug and alcohol addicts.

The programme of Sailaday OK offered an experience to reconnect with external nature as well as our internal nature, allowing a few to perhaps come to recognise the truth – that we *are* nature, which we may deny at great cost not just to ourselves individually but universally.

---

6   Also see ecopsychologists and authors like Paul Shepard 1982 *Nature and Madness* -eco-psychology is a therapeutic technique and ideology that tries to treat people psychologically by bringing them spiritually closer to nature... The term is first used by Theodore Roszak 1992 *The Voice of the Earth*.

2

Splice the Main Brace

Splice the main brace: The Royal Navy discontinued the practice of issuing rum in 1970, but traditionally sailors would 'splice the main brace' for celebrations or as a reward for performing especially onerous duties. A sailor might repay a colleague for a favour by giving him part or all of his grog ration, ranging from 'sippers' (a small amount) via 'gulpers' (a larger quantity) to 'grounders' (the entire tot).

I WAS BORN in 1951, named Richard Philip Hall, and in retrospect I realise today how my life experiences made me the ideal candidate to be the CEO and founder of Sailaday OK (SOK). SOK was a charity, now no longer operating, that offered therapeutic sailing and marine-based adventure therapies for those recovering and having suffered addiction, abuse and trauma, in order to help to reduce disadvantage and social exclusion. I had suffered addiction, abuse and trauma, and by the year 2000 I had been abstinent for five years and was a qualified skipper and psychotherapist.

In the early days of my recovery from chemical addictions, I split my time between living on a boat and looking after a friend's house in St Ives, Cornwall. What I experienced on the boat gave me a head start on others who were in recovery at the same time as me. Two elements were essential in keeping me grounded in my early recovery: this connection with nature, and the activity and the process of sailing which kept me in the here and now – in the present. I had the time and the opportunity, while in isolation from others, to explore my connection to God and nature, and my inner nature; I learned to be comfortable in my skin.

I certainly must have got some of this love of the outdoors from my father. He was a keen sports player (or had been), horse rider and gardener and he taught me how to sail, which is probably the single most important gift he gave me. We used to go down to Cornwall for our summer holidays and there he taught me how to sail dinghies and manage rowing boats and kayaks. I'd like nothing more than just messing about in boats, learning skills, managing risk, and becoming confident when on the water.

My mother educated me about art; at many a mealtime we would be discussing some of the great artists, not just painters, but musicians and ballet dancers. I was even enrolled for a short period with Ballet Rambert. We lived in London and Mum would take me to museums and art galleries and exhibitions. Although she wasn't much in favour of contemporary art, she had a great knowledge of the previous 500 years of art, particularly the 18th and 19th centuries. This blended and integrated well, as my uncle and grandfather on my father's side were well-known marine and landscape painters.

As far back as I can remember I took great pleasure in changing the way I felt. As a youngster playing 'Ring a ring a roses', I would want to play faster and more often than anyone else so that I could enjoy that feeling of being so dizzy I could hardly stand up, so dizzy I would wobble about and then fall over. I found all sorts of other ways of getting that hit, what I would call now that high, that 'out of it' feeling.

As a young teenager I would be invited to parties and sleepovers with friends. There would be drinking and smoking involved, and if there wasn't it wasn't much of a party. I realised that if I woke up early and found all the leftover, part-finished glasses of alcohol and drank them, I would avoid feeling hung over. I considered that a great decision. Similarly, when I drank, I decided I was much more interesting and likeable, which up to a point was probably true, but that behaviour brought me more into the company of others who had made similar decisions, and we could get quite competitive.

I think it must have been somewhere around the early to mid-60s rock 'n' roll era which really grabbed me. My early heroes were Elvis Presley, Cliff Richard, the Everly Brothers and many more. I would listen to them constantly and emulate them as I walked around with my little transistor radio in my ear, much to the annoyance of the rest of my family. And then the Beatles came along, and everybody loved the Beatles, even Mum and Dad, which was one very good reason why I followed the Rolling Stones. They really were *it*, not just the music but what they wore, how they behaved, how they seemed to be putting a finger up to the older generation.

The Rolling Stones took drugs, and the goody-goody Beatles would never do something like that (or so everyone thought at the time), so I remember thinking, this is what I want, this is what I want in my life – sex and drugs and rock 'n' roll. The trouble was, I was still a virgin and I didn't know where to buy any drugs. The best I could do was to pretend to my mates that being a virgin was for wimps, and that if you hadn't smoked pot, you weren't worth being in my gang.

Because I couldn't bear being in anyone else's gang, I had my own gang, and I had to be the leader of that gang. Which also meant I had to be the naughtiest and the most antisocial. This escalating behaviour resulted in being asked to leave my prep school; my Edwardian boarding school, where I was beaten and abused, and then later managing to get thrown out of my public school too at the age of 17.

So, maybe you're beginning to get the picture now of a frustrated and probably angry upper-middle-class boy caught up in the social and cultural changes of the 60s, giving the finger to the past and all that was respectable, predictable, boring and square.

What got me through those school years was a love of sport, the physicality of it and being outdoors, and art – painting, creating and making things. I was good at these and I could lose myself in either of these worlds.

I quickly learned that these were the sorts of activities that pleased people, and in particular my parents. This was a counterbalance to my more disruptive behaviour; an uncle once said these were 'my saving grace'. I also learnt quite early that this was a way to curry favour, to manipulate and to gain an edge on my older brother. I felt as if there was always a competition of who was going to be liked or loved the most, and my survival depended on this. Consequently, I became obsessed with the activities I enjoyed, and which seemed to ingratiate me with my parents – I was driven.

Let's now, briefly, go way back to even earlier formative moments. My first experiences in the womb and post-birth had a profound effect on me. I was rhesus negative which meant firstly that my mother's nutrition in the womb was ineffective, and secondly my blood was no good either. This earliest experience of being between a rock and a hard place, where my very existence was challenged, set up a dynamic that I now think has affected me a great deal in my life. I couldn't live in it and I couldn't live without it. I'm sure that many an addict will recognise that dynamic: 'Can't live with it/ can't live without it'. Those first days, not sure how many there were, I was in an incubator and had to have two total blood transfusions and be revived from death's door more than once.

This sense that my survival was at stake, that my very existence was in question, was an unconscious dynamic that psychologically had a powerful influence on me and may well be the cause of this sense of needing to fight to survive. I had to fight to be loved, to be acknowledged, and I felt that I had been born onto a battlefield. I wonder now, today, writing this, whether there might also have been some genetic, cultural element – something passed down to me from my parents' experience of the previous years of having lived through World War II. They were both thoroughly traumatised and pretty fucked up by the whole experience. Many of my ancestors had been in the military.

I clearly had a strong anti-authoritarian streak in me. I did not like being told what to do, I did not like rules; rules were definitely there to be broken, boundaries to be broken through. It was definitely my job to find the gap, the hole, and to walk the tightrope. There was clearly turmoil, inner conflict and distress, as part of me wanted to be liked and to please. This was the war zone.

My religious education was Protestant, and this meant a weekly visit to church when I was with my parents and more frequently than that when I was at school. From these early days I'd formed a clear picture of this old white-haired bearded man up in heaven judging me. National security would have loved to have had his sophisticated surveillance system because he could even tell what I was thinking. If I was thinking bad thoughts or doing bad things I would go to hell and if I did nice things and be a nice boy I might get to heaven. So, sitting in my Sunday best on the pew with Mum and Dad, trying to look angelic, was a complete contrast to what was going on in my head. I really fancied the girl sitting in front of me – I wanted to put my hand up her skirt or let go of the mouse that I was keeping in my pocket. I would sit there and fantasise all sorts of crazy thoughts until I remembered that God could see everything and I was filled with shame. Shame was as familiar as warm custard.

I acted out being mischievous and naughty to my parents and rebellious with my teachers and schools; I was angry at anyone who tried to tie me down. My strongest memories of my time at those boarding schools is being in fear of being caught; knowing I had done something wrong and was going to be beaten again. But even this dread didn't stop me – I carried on and on and on until I was eventually expelled, consequently confirming my growing conviction that I wasn't really wanted, needed and ultimately proving that my existence was a waste of space. Beatings at school were regular, as well as at home – my mother broke her hairbrush on my arse and used to brag about it to her friends – shame!

I was packed off to boarding school at 7½. Those early years taught me to be self-reliant; I was convinced it was dangerous to let anyone get close, as I would only get hurt. The boarding school environment taught me to be self-sufficient and ambitious and to be highly competitive – that was clearly part of its design and purpose. Everything at school was competitive: your marks in academic subjects, sport, even relationships were competitive. Who would like you most? Who can you manipulate? Who would be bullied or be the bully? Fists and sharp elbows solved most problems in the 'war zone', but I was lonely and isolated.

Thrown out of public school in 1968, what now? Well, Paris awaited me. Paris in June 1968 just happened to be the time and the place for one of the most famous rebellious uprisings of modern times. By sheer luck I had found an exhilarating outlet for rebellion. I joined the student revolution, participating in the riots that nearly brought France to a standstill. Bugger the lofty validations and reasoning of those who wanted a different culture and different world, I just enjoyed the anarchy and chaos. Anti-Vietnam, anti-USA, anti-anything that I, and so many others, could kick against. Back in England, I also got stuck into the student revolts when I was an art student at Guildford Art College which was linked with Hornsey Art College and the London School of Economics. It turned into a whole year of demonstrations and bother.

Guildford Art College couldn't wait to get rid of me. And after my photo appeared in the *Times* newspaper, putting a brick through Maggie Thatcher's window at the Department of Education and Science when she was Minister of Education, Mum and Dad revoked any financial help they had been giving me to help me through college.

No problem! I could always sell drugs; all my friends were at it, and those that weren't selling it were buying it, and even those who were selling it were buying it from somewhere, so it was a brilliant ready-made market waiting to be exploited. Not only that, probably the best part of it of all was that anything I smoked or pills I might have taken were going to be free. I didn't consider myself a drug dealer – I was just a friendly supplier. In my head I was really not doing anything illegal; after all, those that sold alcohol seemed to get drunk and violent and belligerent – they were the ones that should be put in prison. I took on the mantle of the benign hippie, distributing peace and love for £12 an ounce. It was a way of life, a way of making an income that meant I was now an outlaw. I was living outside the law in a world where we made our own rules and regulations. From then on, I always carried my passport with me, ready to flee at any moment, drop everything and go – no ties.

Drugs became my way of life. I really liked being stoned, and it wasn't long before we were selling LSD and taking more volatile drugs. I began mixing with groups who now I guess would be called drug gangs, getting involved in importing and smuggling. Taking hash from Morocco to California and exchanging it for acid crystals which we manufactured into tabs and sold in England. Also involved in a fairly constant supply of hash in North Africa and the Middle East.

This income became enough to survive on, and I found that I could carry on getting my diploma in art and be accepted on a Master's fine art painting course at the Royal Academy. I was certainly straddling two worlds – that of drug culture and, as an RA student, the more acceptable world of fine art. Although I completed my time at the RA and gained my Master's I still didn't feel really satisfied. I realised I was an okay artist, maybe even quite good, but I was never going to be great. I had a moment of clarity when I realised that, as when I was younger when I wanted a world of sex and drugs and rock 'n' roll, I now wanted success. I wanted to be the best at something, to be renowned, to have worldwide recognition. I was still young, arrogant and ambitious, capable and resilient, and I wanted to be adored. I craved recognition, but clearly, I would not be achieving it in the art world.

Along the way, I had been nurturing another source of income, a legal source to explain where my money was coming from. I had become obsessed and knowledgeable about oriental textiles and carpets. This was partly due to coming into contact with others who knew about this market and were exploiting it as cover for importing drugs. Drugs and rugs became my world.

By the mid-70s I was married and had a business partner with a gallery in Little Venice, London where we bought and sold rare oriental textiles and carpets. Our ambition was to take the tribal rug market into the art market, so we bought, sold and exhibited rare and beautiful rugs, kilims and embroideries, which we judged and valued as artworks, not furnishings or even antiques, although they were quite antiquated.

My business partner was also heavily involved in the drugs business and, very willingly, I became involved in bigger smuggling projects. One of our partners was linked to the IRA and, although they profited from the importing and selling marijuana and hash, they had a problem with people dealing with cocaine and other powders. When the IRA realised that we were dealing in cocaine with some of their money we started receiving serious threats. This seemed like a really good time to disappear and get out of London.

The move my wife, Joanna, and I made to a village outside Bath in Somerset was perfect timing also for our plans to have children and to run our textile business to be more orientated around restoration, conservation and consultation. Lannowe Oriental Textiles did eventually become the best-known and the most well-respected privately-run restoration outfit worldwide. But even this wasn't enough, it was never enough.

Cocaine became a big part of my life, and when I couldn't get that I was taking speed. I was also drinking more in the way of spirits and smoking dope all day. Drugs by now were a consistent part of my life. And around this time, I tried heroin, 'brown sugar', 'henry', 'mother's little helper', with pretty disastrous first-time effects: vomiting and passing out. This didn't stop me, and it certainly wasn't enough to put me off. A bit of vomit? Par for the course. One of my clients at this time paid me with 'smack' as they then had a good constant supply. I had a horror of needles, so I only sniffed up my nose, or smoked it – 'chasing the dragon'.

Like our dear friend St George, who was addicted to chasing dragons. He just went from one dragon to the next with a little pause to rescue a maiden. He was also well armoured and protected, so one could never get to know St George or get to see him for who he really was. As you can tell I sort of identified with St George.

Over the next 20 years I became a father of three children and an employer of 15 to 20 men and women, who were the workforce in our restoration and conservation business. Lannowe Oriental Textiles became an international business and was regarded as the best independent business of its kind in the world. I had achieved my goal, but unfortunately, yet again, I didn't feel satisfied. In fact, by this stage in my life nothing was enough. I was a functioning addict.

Over this period, all my addictions flourished: workaholic, adrenaline junkie, and a continuous balancing act of one drug taking me up and another one to bring me down. I was walking a permanent tightrope in order to remain functioning to some degree or other. Add to this toxic mix a sex addiction that was based on the belief that the quantity and quality of sex was the measure of a good relationship. Words like intimacy, vulnerability, closeness and love didn't really seem to come into it. It wasn't until much later that I learnt about the word co-dependency. I thought it was normal to feel that I was only complete, only whole, when I was in a woman's arms. I was addicted to work; the business was international which meant we were open seven days a week, 24 hours a day. Oh, and I was also addicted to debt, and so all in all I was pretty messed up.

By the age of 40 I had suffered my first near-death experience and hospitalisation after overdosing. I was often physically ill from too much alcohol, periods of withdrawal and the pain from not enough heroin. I was frequently despairing and suicidal; I blamed everyone else for my difficulties and took very little responsibility for the state I got myself into. It was only just dawning on me that I might have a problem. Up to that point I was convinced that I just liked taking drugs a little bit more than a few other people. The acquiring and consuming of drugs and alcohol was my priority, my main ambition for each day. Everything else was peripheral, everything else came second, including my relationship with my wife and children, the business and our social standing in the community. Sometime back then, a girl friend who I really liked said to me how much nicer I was when I wasn't stoned. How weird was that – I couldn't get my head around it. I felt insecure, inadequate and anxious when not stoned.

The next five years were agony: I couldn't live with it and I couldn't live without it. I hated whom I had become, and none of the tricks I was using to lessen my intake seemed to work. I tried changing my intake, switching drugs and alcohol, not starting till midday. I was on a methadone prescription and still spending about a thousand pounds a week – in 1993 that was a *lot* of money. I was becoming very ill and had begun to think I might need some help, as I could no longer do this on my own.

One more overdose, one more hospitalisation, the stomach pump again, and twice they had to get my heart going again while in the ambulance. I spent the day in hospital in Bath and before I was discharged the psychiatrist interviewed me.

He asked me, "Was this a suicide attempt?" I replied, "No, it was just recreational".

This was completely nuts and it only got worse, I had to do something. I needed help and I decided to try an addiction rehabilitation treatment centre. The one I liked the look of most was a place called Clouds in Wiltshire. I booked myself in for six weeks, which seemed an excessive amount of time. I thought I should be fine after only a couple of weeks, and I was a bit miffed that I couldn't take any books or my pet rat. In fact, I didn't have a clue; I had no idea what I was letting myself in for. I thought I was going to a health spa; it looked like a health spa, a nice big country home in beautiful countryside.

They say that withdrawal from methadone is probably the most painful of all withdrawals, and the first ten days were indeed agony – I was in pain right down inside, into the marrow of my bones. During the next couple of weeks I began to learn a little bit about my condition; I began to learn that there was such a thing called recovery and that successful recovery needed abstinence. Abstinence from everything chemical – "What? Wow!" I began to participate in the therapy and began to even like and enjoy the group therapy as long as it wasn't focused on me. I became adept at avoiding scrutiny by maintaining the camouflage / armour plating necessary to hide.

By looking, appearing and sounding willing, I managed to hide my real self; I could keep my secrets.

The Clouds residential centre used the 12-Step Programme[1] as part of its treatment, involving going to AA (Alcoholics Anonymous), and NA (Narcotics Anonymous) meetings at least twice, if not three times, a week. These were evening meetings somewhere in the neighbourhood, which we were bussed to, the furthest being Salisbury. I knew several dealers in Salisbury, and it was very tempting to go AWOL and score, but I didn't. However, I did end up in a fight over a game of chess, chasing my antagonist around the house with a carving knife while he had armed himself with a croquet mallet. We were both expelled, what a surprise!

I continued to attend AA and NA meetings mostly in Bath and Bristol and I began to listen and to hear that there were other people not that dissimilar from me. Although, of course, I had never done half of what they had done, or said they had done. I was pretty convinced that I was special and different, or I felt I had to compete and tell even bigger war stories. However, I guess it was a beginning, a way to start unravelling and processing some of the trauma. When I did listen, the fact that these were both spiritual programmes started to make real sense to me. It was not just a set of rules that had to be adhered to, but it was about making a connection to something bigger than ourselves. I had always considered myself the most important person; everything revolved around me. My narcissism was rampant, being well fed by chemicals. When taking LSD my biggest desire was to meet God, but when I did meet him, I realised it was me, I was God. Without the chemicals to keep this fantasy going, I began to fall apart and fragment, resulting in a relapse that lasted another year. I would go to AA having used drugs, and go to NA having used alcohol; of course, I was kosher for not having drunk at an AA meeting and then playing the other trick at NA meetings. Keeping all these lies going and all these balls in the air. I was facing the incredibly gruesome dilemma that I was going to die if I stopped taking, and I was going to die if I didn't stop.

I tried residential therapy again, back at Clouds, and this time I completed the six weeks. I really began to get a glimmer of what recovery could be about; I began to get a sense of a whole new world waiting to be discovered, and this was frightening and exhilarating. I threw myself into the 12-Step programme and did everything I could to make it a success. I worked hard at all the projects and written work. If I had been marked out of 10, I hope

---

1   12-Step programme: for mutual aid, self-help, organisations whose purpose is to aid recovering from a variety of addictions. AA: Alcoholics Anonymous; NA: Narcotics Anonymous and so forth.

I would have been given at least 9/10 – none of this "you could do better" business. I began to feel a little bit sane and with this came the realisation that I had been quite insane – absolutely bonkers.

This enormous effort, this fight to stay clean, was not the true journey to recovery, as it did not acknowledge two vital ingredients – acceptance and surrender. Consequently, it wasn't long before I relapsed.

At this time, I had a sponsor in Bath, and he did his best to encourage me to keep going to self-help fellowship meetings of the anonymous kind, but I came to expect a lot more from him than that. I expected him to make it all go away. I wanted it now. He had made it go away for him so why couldn't he make it go away for me. I would arrive at his house raving, snivelling and crying and feeling suicidal, telling him I couldn't bear this feeling any longer and that I expected miracles from him. He would drive me completely bonkers by repeating this same sentence: "The feelings won't kill you but the chemicals will." "Bollocks", I thought, but I kept going back.

I even decided to go back home after my success at Clouds and tried to adopt a new lifestyle, a clean and spiritual way of life. This was really hard, as hard as stopping taking chemicals. I had to have a completely new and fresh relationship with my children. I didn't know what I felt towards Joanna although I desperately needed her, and work was overwhelming. I tried terribly hard to make changes in all these different areas of my life.

They say that at different stages in your recovery you will be tested. I was surely tested by my parents or my parents' situation. Dad was becoming increasingly ill and in pain and ricocheted between residential care, hospital care and useless care from my mother. Without Dad, Mum retreated into alcohol, prescribed drugs and suicide attempts. I felt so powerless watching them slide towards death. Dad died in great pain, barely conscious, and a few months after that Mum followed, in a residential home where she managed to swallow enough medication so that she had a heart attack and died. My immediate reaction was not grief but a great sense of relief, not just that they were out of pain, but out of my life and I could now get on with it. I could be the person I wanted to be, not the one I thought that they wanted me to be. It's taken many years of therapy to overcome the guilt of those feelings, the fantastic feeling of freedom that they had gone.

This was followed by a death-defying spiral of extreme drinking; I had several near-death experiences and how I didn't actually die is a complete miracle. But I did manage to get myself into treatment in Clouds once more, but within a few days I was expelled yet again for hiding my medication in my palm instead of taking it. Places like this rely on trust and I had abused that.

I went home that weekend with three phone numbers of other residential centres that might take me. The third one I rang gave me an intake over the phone and told me if I got there by Monday, I could have a place – "there" being Plymouth.

Some weeks before, I had visited a long-term secondary rehab centre in Cornwall called Bosence. They told me that if I was clean for three months, they would give me a place, for an unlimited time. After talking about my history, they advised that I should be there for anything from six months to 2 years, but I would have to pay for it myself. If I was accepted for state benefits that would be sufficient to confirm my place, and I had to ring them up once a week from Plymouth and tell them how I was getting on.

One winter morning in 1997, Joanna took me to Bath station, put me on a train to Plymouth, and gave me enough cash for me to get to the address of the residential centre, which was written down on a scrap of paper. On the station we said our goodbyes; I was pretty confused and emotional. Joanna asked me how long did I think this would take before I came home. I told her that I didn't know, and her reply still rings in my ears: *"Well, if you don't know then don't bother to come back"*.

I arrived at Broadreach Residential Centre[2], incontinent, unable to get up one flight of stairs without resting, couldn't drink a cup of tea without spilling half of it, couldn't get anything to stay on a fork as I was shaking so much, so had to eat with a spoon. It was incredibly painful to stay for one hour of group therapy. I couldn't sleep, didn't know what I was thinking or feeling except pain, anger, rage and a world of shame which I hid in my hoody. Everything ached, from mild irritation and discomfort to agonies of cramps that seemed to come from deep, deep within me. It was my bones – my very core was on fire, and in the rare moments that I could think, I thought, "I'm dying".

---

2   Broadreach: residential primary addiction recovery centre, primary care for 6 weeks, Plymouth.

3

Under the Weather

*Under the weather: serving a watch on the weather
side of the ship, exposed to wind and spray.*

THE SUMMER BEFORE I went into Broadreach residential centre, I spent a fair amount of time on my small boat moored at Helford near Falmouth. Some of this time was spent with my two boys, but mostly it was a good opportunity to drink on my own. When capable, I would get to AA in Falmouth, where I made various friends. One of them was a keen sailor who used to come out with me for the occasional day-sail. One day, we were out sailing talking about recovery and the fellowship and she said to me, "Richard, when are you going to surrender?"

Before I had time to think about it, I blurted out, "I don't know how". There was a long pause, and we both realised what an important statement this was. I knew how to try hard, but I didn't know how to roll over, give up, stop trying and surrender. I sort of understood that this was a major part of recovery – acceptance that I was an addict and an alcoholic and that I needed to surrender. The act of making that statement opened the door, increased my awareness and suddenly part of the jigsaw fell into place. I needed help and I had finally come to understand that I needed to be shown "how to surrender." How did you do that, what did that look like, and how did that feel?

There was one other major event that changed everything in those last desperate days before committing myself to Broadreach. Over that period of just four months both my parents had died. Death was familiar; I could almost call it a friend, and at times I even welcomed death – I certainly courted death. Having clinically died on more than one occasion (and having been revived) must have had some impact on me, but on a conscious level I was in denial. My parents dying within such a short space of time was dramatic, and these events confronted my denial, but also set me free. I guess that there was a recognition of what death is – my parents weren't coming back, they weren't going to be revived. I had got away with it a few times, I'd stared into the abyss and I'd been to some very dark places, but this made me confront the fact that this didn't mean that I was always going to bounce back. Contemplating these events took me to the edge, into the darkest of places, where no light existed. Down deep in there I touched base, experienced an incredible force, a great urge, like a bubble of air charging towards the surface. I now felt this drive to live – I wanted to live. "I wanted to live!" – I had never voiced this before. I had had a huge appetite for living but had never accepted my aliveness, but at this point I made a conscious decision that I wanted to live, I was going to do whatever it took to live and to live well.

When I arrived at Broadreach, I felt completely beaten and was extremely ill. I was occasionally incontinent and completely incompetent at living. I was just under six feet tall, weighed 7½ stone, and my eyes and teeth were in a terrible state. It was almost impossible for me to focus on what was being said and to follow a conversation, and I was ready to surrender. I was at the starting point, and even though I had nothing left inside me to fight with, I was prepared to go to any lengths to live.

I couldn't imagine what sort of quality of life I might have in the future; I was told to live one day at a time but at that time I could barely live one cigarette at a time, one cup of tea at a time. This slowly expanded to a meal at a time and so on, and so on, until I could begin to imagine a whole day ahead of me. The most overwhelming emotion I felt was grief; I would burst into tears at any moment and once I started, I thought I would never stop. I was told that this was normal and healthy, but it didn't feel healthy; I felt so ashamed of myself and was in a state of permanent high anxiety and agitation.

We would have group time, group therapy, and one-to-one time with our primary counsellor. There were different sorts of groups: male only groups and, of course, female only groups. There were also family groups, harm and denial groups and, being fellowship orientated, there would be Step groups, exploring the 12 different steps of the recovery fellowship.

My counsellor, Josey, was a star and she very quickly came to understand me in a way I found difficult to comprehend. I would wait outside her office every morning when she came into work and beg her to give me some sort of an assignment, a project, something I could get my teeth stuck into.

Something I could worry to death and avoid being me. She would refuse and tell me to socialise, get to know myself and stop trying so hard. This was bloody agony as the last thing I wanted to do was explore myself. However, I followed her advice and reluctantly prospered.

This was all part of the process of surrendering and accepting, taking account of what we've done to ourselves and to others and understanding that there were others who have trodden this path before us with success, so we need to walk in their footsteps. I also came to understand that change is the essence of recovery.

I didn't just need to change my behaviour; I also needed to change my attitude and bring my belief system up to date. I began to achieve some clarity about my experiences in the past when I had left residential centres and had tried, tried so terribly hard to get my family, my job and my work all back together again. This didn't work for me; I couldn't go back, I needed to change everything. I had had to walk away from my family, and I hadn't really begun to explore the shame in that. I also had to turn my back on the business I had created, as well as my home, my car and all the artefacts that surrounded me at home. My pride, my ego and my image had deserted me, leaving me bereft, a husk, containing shame and guilt and the agonising knowledge that I had abandoned my children. I couldn't bear the truth that I had abandoned them and was in so much denial that I could rationalise that it was for their own good. I had walked out on them and justified it by saying that they were better off without me, and I was clearly going to die if I had stayed.

However, the truth is that I abandoned them to regain my life, but in doing so, I had scarred my children.

I kept checking in with Bosence Farm[1] and was fairly sure I had a place there after Christmas. I was still at Broadreach in Plymouth at Christmas and that was a difficult time. A lot of letting go; a lot of yearning and grief and the recognition that if I went down to Cornwall with no fixed time limit, this would be the last straw and probably the end of my marriage. I would be burning my bridges. I was at least well supported by the therapy team and my peers – the other alcoholics and addicts who were struggling together with me. This gave me the strength to stay on the path and maintain my recovery, overriding any doubts, because I knew that if I wanted to live, I needed to do this thing.

A week after New Year's Day I went down to Cornwall and was given my own little room at Bosence Farm. The centre had hardly been running

---

[1] Bosence Farm, Cornwall, secondary addiction recovery centre, eight weeks to 2 years.

for a year and was not very well equipped. There were ten of us residents and only two fan heaters; these we had to share around, taking turns on different nights. There was no central heating, no television or other distractions; nothing to hide behind. However, there was plenty to eat and, most importantly, a great atmosphere of love and mutual support. Bosence Farm is in the middle of the countryside, quite remote and beautiful, and I felt I had gone through a long dark tunnel and had arrived at this heavenly destination. Here I could find some peace, take on the work I needed to do, and recover.

Some years back, I remember a good and dear friend who understood my condition, and who also sometimes treated me with acupuncture therapy, asked me what I really wanted. I felt completely tongue-tied and incapable of answering and came out with a rather feeble reply like a bigger house, a boat, maybe more time with my family. He didn't say anything, but I knew this wasn't really what he was asking me. At Bosence Farm I began to explore that question and, given my new state of mind and body, I came to the conclusion that what I really would like above all else would be to find some peace, and this became my goal. I came to understand that if I worked the Steps, accepted my part in my past and learned forgiveness, I might achieve peace. I threw myself upon the fellowships and immersed myself in following the 12-Step programme, going to meetings four or five times a week. I got stuck in, did service, became part of it and began to feel that I belonged.

There was another frequently asked question; the sort of question an earthling would ask: "When will you have had enough Richard?", but I could not answer. It felt like a trap, a trick question – I couldn't really admit that I could never get enough. Of course, when I did admit it, and accepted that I could never get enough, this truth set me free and never again did I need to attempt to fill that bottomless, deep and dismal hole. I just needed to look the other way, move towards the light and keep it really simple. God, was it that simple? Was it really that easy? If anything became difficult to achieve, it was simply that I was looking in the wrong direction. I didn't have to try hard anymore, all I had to do was let go. Welcome, ease and peace.

Every day I would walk as far as I was allowed, and just spend time in the countryside, immersing myself in nature. Very often I would just stand and watch the world around me, allowing all the jabber in my head to unravel, just letting it go, and connecting. This took effort, it wasn't easy, doing nothing, it took commitment and dedication. The programme at Bosence was carefully designed so that we couldn't hide away in other activities, like a gym or mobile phones or sexual relationships. This didn't suit everybody but was perfect for me, and what I did see over and over again was people getting involved in relationships, and subsequently relapsing. A clear warning to me.

After six months at Bosence Farm my money had run out, and I'd been offered a place to stay in St Ives, looking after a friend's house while he was away for six months. During the last months at Bosence I had been given increased freedom, including buying a small car to visit my boat and start cleaning it up with a view to living on her. However, this offer to stay in St Ives let me have my cake and eat it. I had a base in a town where I could keep in contact with Bosence Farm and maintain all my commitments to the fellowships. I also had my own space and retreat in the old boat called *Odd Socks* along with my friend, Ratty the pet rat.

On my first day of 'freedom' I received a letter from my wife, Joanna, telling me that she had found some other male mate and wanted a divorce; all my paranoid fantasies had come true. Often, I had been told that I would be tested, and my God what a test. I needed to put into practice everything I had been taught. I needed to get to a meeting, talk to people, tell them what I was feeling, get vulnerable, get real and ask for help.

I had often fantasised that Joanna would find someone else, and this just fed my self-absorption, grief and rage, and I would end up wanting to kill her and possibly the other. There was also a strong erotic urge when thinking of her with somebody else and this felt quite shameful. I had also been told that I would only be tested as far as I was capable and that I was resilient enough to survive. This was proving to be some test and I thought I'd done more than survive, as I began to find some more equilibrium and balance in this new situation. I felt I'd moved on, I wasn't stuck. I felt a great sense of gratitude and understanding.

Part of the 12-Step programme was to find a sponsor, someone you could identify with, and with whom there was empathy and mutual liking and understanding. This person was to be a sort of mentor, guiding you through the Steps and enhancing your recovery. I did find a sponsor, K, and he really helped me interpret the Steps and helped to make other literature more meaningful for me. I was attracted to this person because he spoke so boldly about God, about the damage done to our spirit and soul when in active addiction, and how we could be guided when we listened and prayed for the healing of these deep wounds. At our first meeting I talked about my occasional feelings of craving, and certainly about having dreams about using, as I was having thoughts about having a drink or scoring. He asked me if I ever prayed and I talked about my humble mumblings while in bed before going to sleep and when I got up in the morning. He advised me very strongly if I were to pray, I was to fully commit myself – I was to get on my knees, surrender myself to God, bow down and then pray. I was a little reluctant at first, even resistant. However, I had committed to do anything, go to any lengths, and so I practised praying. I felt great release when getting down on my knees, lowering my head, touching my head to the floor and surrendering to God and to His will. On one occasion around that time, I asked for help about my cravings, I asked for them to be taken away. I said very clearly, they were not what I wanted, I wanted clarity of vision, and I wanted to do God's will. From that moment on I never felt a craving again. Yes, really, it happened just like that. I am at a loss to explain how that is possible, how it came to pass other than the power of prayer.

I had a caring and loving relationship with my sponsor, although I struggled with what I viewed as inequality. I understood he was also recovering and spoke from a good place, not wanting to put me down, but I resented his authority over me, and we finally parted company. I had started to undertake some training in psychotherapy and had met a woman I wanted to know better. I felt too that she wanted to know me better – we were also at a starting place. Poor K, my sponsor, declared that I was far too wilful for him and he had to let me go.

During the various treatments and residential sessions, I had attended, and thoroughly and fearlessly taken part in, group and one-to-one therapy. Some of the counsellors were better than others. Some were mere beginners, recovering addicts themselves, but some were highly skilled, and I really wanted to know how they managed to facilitate the changes I made in my behaviour, my attitudes and beliefs. I realise how hard I had resisted them in the beginning, and yet they persevered and used this energy to help increase my awareness, my self-awareness, and to help me dig deep down into the parts that I found hard to know – the areas I kept safely locked away in the dark. I had this sense that they were prepared to travel with me and this was comforting and encouraging. They had great empathy.

I guess, to begin with, I just desired to be like them, and then I began to read and explore different forms of counselling and discover the difference between counselling and psychotherapy. I tried a couple of different therapists when I could afford it and came to a conclusion that the one programme I liked best was Transactional Analysis.[2] I joined a therapy group run by a transactional analyst and was fascinated to find that there were other people with just as disfiguring personality difficulties as myself, even without being addicts. This therapist also ran training sessions, and

---

2   Transactional Analysis; Transactional Analysts: TA is a cycle therapeutic theory and method of therapy wherein social transactions are analysed to determine the ego state of the communication: parent-like, childlike or adult-like, as a basis for understanding behaviour.

I made a highly tentative start by helping to run some weekend training groups. Being involved in any training sessions in psychotherapy, part of the training entails practising within the group (including oneself), and with the trainer, which meant I was also getting a great deal more therapy that I normally could have been able to afford.

While at Bosence Farm I had practised yoga and Tai Chi, and I had met somebody at the Tai Chi classes who called themselves a Reiki Master.[3] This intrigued me, and I wanted to know more about what she did. I was at times suffering quite bad back pains, an old injury that would flare up now and again. I had tried various osteopaths, acupuncture and other treatments for a large part of my life, none of which had been very effective and certainly not long lasting. The Reiki Master offered me a free treatment, to give me a sample of this form of healing, which uses Chi energy through the laying on of hands and directing one's intent, one's energy towards the issue that might need healing. After two treatments my back was remarkably improved, so I started on a series of training with another Reiki Master who taught me many of the secrets of this form of universal energy healing, treating the physical, psychological and emotional.

As I began to practise this form of therapy, I was initiated into the different stages until I could become a Reiki Master myself. The trick was to tune into another person's energy fields. Laying on of hands is a traditional form of healing across millennia in Christian, Jewish and spiritualist traditions. The recipient responds through shifts in the body's energy, primarily brought about via touch. Reiki is energy healing; practitioners use a technique called palm healing, or hands-on healing through which universal energy is said to be transferred through the palms of the practitioner to the patient, to bring about and encourage emotional or physical healing.

As I became more experienced, I came to understand that these shifts in energy didn't even necessarily need this hands-on approach. I began to detect that there were various energy shifts occurring within the client even when they were participating in more traditional therapy or psychotherapy. I also began to realise that my own body responded to these changes, and by listening to my body and tuning into my empathic responses to the other person on a sensory level, I could identify some of the upheavals, splitting, and general disturbance in the other, quite often long before they recognised it themselves. This was quite a revelation and it was fascinating to detect and channel this shared energy.

---

3   Reiki: a Japanese form of alternative medicine called energy healing, Reiki practitioners use a technique called palm healing or hands-on healing.

I also found it fascinating that my sailing skills greatly improved if I allowed myself to connect to the environment around me using similar (Reiki) techniques. My wind awareness, my relationship to the sea and all the pressures and changes it was exerting on the boat, and consequently my connection to the boat, were greatly enhanced. In short, I found I could connect to the marine environment with much greater ease. By this process of unifying, I felt a part of, and intimately connected to, the environment. The truth of the matter was that I was learning to connect with my inner nature, as well as the nature and marine environment around me, and this was a primal experience.

I was spending at least half of each week on the boat; sometimes sailing to a destination maybe 20 or 30 miles away up the coast, but mostly pottering around in Falmouth Bay exploring the surrounding coastlines. Most of the anchorages were quiet, beautiful places – small bays and wooded creeks. Depending on the weather conditions each one had its advantages and disadvantages. When in Falmouth, I could re-provision and make it to a fellowship meeting, so it was pretty idyllic.

Improving my proficiency at sailing, practising sailing skills and management of a boat, and resolving problems on my own, learning self-sufficiency, were all part of the process. Introspection and long periods of contemplation and meditation were my primary focus. Developing and exploring this connection to my inner self, my inner spirit, was bringing about a state of transition. Being on my own in such a beautiful natural environment, even when it got windy, wet and stormy, was transformative.

I alternated between feeling enormous gratitude and pleasure and experiencing dark and painful days and nights, full of tears and doubts. I realised that by staying longer connected to these painful sensations I could explore them more deeply. At times they were accompanied by physical sensations; aches and pains cropping up in one part of my body and then moving onto somewhere else. Terrible headaches would shift down to my shoulders and then down to the bottom of my back and my hips. If I allowed these aches and pains to exist and accept them, they would morph into some other sensation, probably somewhere else in my body. As I became more adept at doing this, I accepted them for exactly what they were. I was not trying to make them mean anything, just maybe accepting them as something important, as though I was being shown something. I was being prised open like an oyster to reveal the luscious fruit within. As this process continued, I began to sense that it was a battle going on, a battle raging within me. Something was being resisted, some part of me was resisting with everything I had not to go there, not to feel this or that, not to allow myself down into the deep dark bleak blackness some may describe as the dark night of the soul. The word that came to mind eventually was 'shame'. Not just a shame of what I had done or been, but a shame of having existed at all. It was as if that first experience of life was undeserved, that there was something basically wrong with me. I was suffering from shame, from the original sin of being. Throughout my years of addictions, I had certainly proved to others that I wasn't worth it, that my existence was a negative. So, I came to understand the depths I had reached and this proved my unworthiness to exist. Time to forgive, time to move on; time to say goodbye to the monkey on my back. But that wouldn't be easy – he had his claws deep into me and there was going to be blood and gore to tear them out and away.

As soon as this became clearer in my mind and I could put it into words by writing it down in my journal, I felt I was making room for even more acceptance, happiness, peace and rightness. I guess, at that time, the idea of feeling joy was way beyond my capability, but what I did crave was to just feel okay. Okay with me and okay with the world around me. I realised I had reached another jumping off place, as another door had been opened. The challenge now was whether I was I prepared to walk through the door, dive into the pool, and commit to the unknown.

I began to recognise that a different, an alternative personality was emerging, enhanced by this way of being and that these changes were greatly improved by sailing and just being in this environment. Sailing calls for greater awareness of the present conditions around you, the environment, and one's own condition. One needs to be very present, very much in the here and now, able to respond to the changes and adapt to environmental fluctuations. Clearly, when the wind changed, I needed to adapt, but likewise I also needed to make changes if I felt cold or needed to eat.

When in active addiction, the last place I had wanted to be was in the present – in the here and now; my mind was either in the past or in the future. The present felt like a great weight of self-hatred and anger, rage against the world around me, but mostly raging at me and consequently trying to annihilate me. Oblivion had been the target; unconsciousness was a preferable state of mind to be in. Raking up the past and blaming everybody else for my ills and problems, being a victim had been my preferred state of mind and behaviour. And worse than that, when not playing the victim I would dash out from my hiding place and create great dramas to hide behind and then persecute those that cared for me.

I was undergoing great life-enhancing changes; I felt like a butterfly emerging from its chrysalis. You may know the story about the man who spoke to the larva or chrysalis and told it how it was about to become a beautiful, colourful graceful creature, with the gift of flight. The chrysalis replied, but there are various versions of what it may have said. "You're talking load of bollocks" might have been one of them. Emerging from the pupae must have been a painful experience, as the skin splits and you have to climb out, squeeze your way out of this sticky world. The past is painfully stuck to you and attempting to hold you from becoming what nature ordained. I think I prefer, as a metaphor of change, that of alchemy, where raw base metals are subjected to great heat and are turned into gold. Some of those nights on *Odd Socks* were not dissimilar. The past had stuck to me and however I twisted and turned it just seem to stay latched on and burned its way into me. But ultimately, it was an alchemical, cleansing process, with some glimmers of gold in sight.

The thought increasingly occurred to me that what I was experiencing might be useful for many other people, as it might be a route out of addiction for others. Through sailing I was learning about my inner nature: I was becoming more resilient, more self-aware, more empathic, and learning to enjoy just being in the present, in the here and now.

I became more accustomed to this process and recognised the benefits and was more aware of the changes that were taking place inside me as well as my altered attitude to the world around me. As I became more accepting of myself, I hesitate to use the word loving, but I must have grown closer to love. As I became more at ease with being me, it became easier for others to be with me. As the scales and camouflage fell away, I became more visible and I think, I hope, more attractive to others.

4

Son of a Gun

Son of a gun: *The space between the guns was used as a semi-private place for trysts with prostitutes and wives, which sometimes led to the birth of children with disputed parentage. Another theory is that the origin the term derived from the firing of a ship's guns to hasten a difficult birth.*

IT WAS LOVE that brought Sue and me together, and around that time I moved into Sue's house, just outside St Ives. I sold *Odd Socks* as I needed a bigger boat for us to go adventuring in. I bought *Serenade*, a 27-foot twin bilge keel, four-berth McWester yacht. I also landed my first paid job as a psychotherapist and, having set up a base at Carbis Bay, I could develop my private practice.

This sense of loving and being loved was the food I really craved. Suddenly I was in the flow of a life force that healed all. I had recovered and matured enough to accept love and know that I was loved, warts and all. This was revolutionary; this was a whole new way of living. I had never had a relationship like this before, where love came first and sex came second. In all my other relationships it had been the other way around. Sue and I were not alike – we didn't agree on everything; she wasn't the other half that made my life whole, but we were in love and she was my lover.

Sue had had a private practice as a counsellor for some years, but we now completed our psychotherapy training together in Cornwall. There was a lot to share and discuss and compare notes as therapists as well as on a personal basis. We shared and explored books by Deepak

Chopra[1] who wrote about metaphysics in the study of consciousness and the "dynamically active consciousness" which he would say is a fundamental feature of the universe. Also, Marianne Williamson's *Return to Love*. I could so easily identify with her opening statement: "Our deepest fear is not that we are inadequate. Our deepest fear is that we are powerful beyond measure". Another book, *The Course of Miracles*[2] opened many doors for us both. Also, we both practised Reiki.

In this new environment I thrived spiritually, emotionally and physically. The past began to fall into place, and I began to get a better perspective on the present. The parts of me that had felt fragmented, as in a jigsaw, started to join up and I began to see a complete picture. I felt my feet were more firmly on the ground, even when I was on the boat.

Time on my own sailing was part of my weekly programme, and so much was changing within and without. Although it was necessary to process a lot with Sue, I also needed time on my own or I would become overwhelmed, fearful and anxious. When this happened, I got angry and defensive.

I was really pleased to finally get paid as a psychotherapist by Bosence Farm Residential Centre as a standby therapist, where I would run groups and work one-to-one with some of the residents. To start with I was on the occasional day or few days as standby therapist. I began to be valued as a psychotherapist and I was invited more and more often to take the place of the other counsellors when they were struck by illness or taking holidays. This meant that I might be working there two weeks or so at a time, and this gave me the opportunity to build deeper and more meaningful relationships with the residents.

I would have one-to-one sessions with an individual if his or her primary counsellor was away, but more regularly I would take therapy groups. These may have involved anything up to 10 or 12 people at a time. I surprised myself by being at ease running these groups and finding that I really enjoyed them. It became obvious that many of the residents had similar histories to me and they appreciated my empathy. There were differences, but also a great many similarities. The most obvious were difficulties in coming to terms with our changes in behaviour and attitudes in recovery; the emotional mental processes involved in recovery. It was often hard for some to understand that

---

1   Deepak Chopra: *Seven Spiritual Laws of Success* ASIN B005BY3XHC, is Indian-American and an alternative medicine advocate. He is a prominent figure in the New Age movement; he is said to have stated, "Your mind and body and your consciousness, your spirit and your social interactions, your personal relationships, your environment, and how you deal with the environment and your biology, are all in inextricably woven into a single process."

2   *The Course of Miracles* ASIN B00J7VUL91 1976 by Helen Schucman. In the workbook version she presents 365 lessons, one for each day of the year. And see also: Marianne Williamson *A Return to Love* ISBN 9780722532997

they had changed; they were often stuck with thinking they were who they used to be, and they needed encouragement to throw off the old mantle and take on the new. To shed the old skin and welcome the new, even if it was a bit tight and itchy. They came to trust me, and consequently we could move more smoothly and deeply into the issues that were troubling them. If they were prepared to take a risk and let themselves become more vulnerable, this could be a great step forward in their recovery. I came to recognise that my history and recovery was not something to be ashamed of but was of real value and benefit to others. The staff at Bosence also recognised my value, as my age and history were important in this process.

In the afternoons and weekends there was plenty of spare time. They might have other projects going on like pottery, yoga or working in the grounds and garden. I enjoyed the outdoor activities, such as taking them on walks in the Cornish countryside, taking them to fabulous places along cliffs and seaside, remote highlands and hidden woodlands. There was one occasion, when walking through Falmouth, that one of them mentioned how amazing it would be to go out on a boat and see the world from a different place. To get a different perspective, to see the world from the outside. This was like a rocket going off in my head. The thought rattled around my head for several days: '...why not take them out for a day on *Serenade?*'

There had already been occasions, during the winter, when I might have taken one or two people down to help me work on the boat when she was at Gweek, where she was laid up, and they would help to get her prepared for the coming season. So, I had already proved that I was trustworthy enough to take some residents out for a day on my own, and it wasn't too big a stretch for management to agree that I might take two or more for a day's sailing.

So, this is how it all started, this was the step that changed everything: the path to Sailaday OK. I didn't know it at the time; it just seemed like a good idea, and an organic process. I would decide a day at a weekend, with suitable weather and the right tides. I didn't want to terrify everybody, and I didn't want a boat full of seasick traumatised residents, so I was cautious and highly safety conscious.

I took the first group of three out for a day on a Saturday. Most of Sunday they were still talking about it, telling everybody what a great experience it had been. Monday morning, they couldn't stop themselves from telling the staff over and over what a fab time they had had. They talked about how well they felt after a day out at sea; they talked with excitement about how they had been in charge of the boat and done some steering and 'tacking'. They were amazed that I had trusted them when motoring or sailing and had let them be 'in charge' of the boat, or apparently in charge. I say apparently because I kept a careful eye on them and a weather eye on the environment to keep it safe. I must have done this successfully and without showing any tension or anxiety. It all felt easy; there was plenty of laughter and goodwill. One of the other things they kept saying over and over again was how excited they were to have had a day that was fun, novel, even a little frightening at times, but that they hadn't been using. They had had fun without drugs and alcohol. They had taken a little risk, learned something new and, like all good addicts, they wanted to do it again and again and again.

This experience also gave me a lot to think about and I started to talk about how to enrich and enhance it. At that time, I was reading about experiential education, and writings by Jung, the psychologist and psychoanalyst: "It is likely that one cannot understand a thing until we have experienced it inwardly." This was experiential learning by having an adventure. What could be healthier than a day out at sea, learning about sailing, nature, and oneself?

I realised that these first few outings were trials towards something better. This activity was worth developing, but I also had a head full of questions, specifically how to integrate this experience so that it wasn't just a jolly day out. From my experience of sailing and being in that environment I understood the positive changes that came about for me. I loved sailing and I was passionate about it because the experience wasn't in isolation to the rest of my life – the changes in my whole psyche and my soul didn't just stop when I stepped off the boat. The experience had a profound effect upon my ability to function ashore. Over a short period of time, I had improved my ability to form relationships and become open, true and honest with myself and others. I felt more grounded and more developed. I felt like an adult, a grown-up person able to take on life on its own terms.

The big question was, how could I help these participants embed the experience, how could this be integrated into the rest of their lives? This seemed to be the key issue to resolve to help turn the activity from just a jolly, a nice day out, a bit of a holiday, into a profound life-changing experience.

Having spoken to other psychotherapists and in particular Sue, I realised the answer might be found somewhere in my psychotherapy textbooks. I had to look to my training as a transactional analyst, which looks upon every transaction, and in particular every verbal transaction, as of great importance. Transactional analysis concentrates not so much on the content as the underlying process of people's interactions with each other. This helped me to understand that there is a shift in attention between the external and the internal dialogue. Hearing the words spoken consciously has an impact on our unconscious. If I just think to myself, 'what a nice day

I had on the boat', it doesn't go very deep and has very little impact on my unconscious self. However, if I tell someone, "I had a great day out because I enjoyed the activity and now I feel relaxed and pleasantly tired", the whole experience is compounded, strengthened and enhanced. If I then increase this dialogue by saying, "The whole experience has made me feel far more confident", it becomes even more meaningful.

The originator of transactional analysis, Eric Berne, believed that insights could be better discovered by analysing the patient's social transactions. Berne matched interpersonal relationships to three ego states of the individual: the parent, adult and child ego states. Most people with psychological issues will not have a fully functioning adult ego state. Learning to strengthen the adult is a goal for most transactional analysis psychotherapists. If a person is directed towards an objective appraisal of reality whilst in their adult ego state, they are more likely to function better in the here and now.

It became clear to me that the very activity of sailing had a highly beneficial effect on one's adult ego state, because sailing is so much about being in the here and now, making decisions and resolving problems that are manifested in the present. This is about increasing one's personal awareness of one's own condition and reacting and adapting to the conditions that are constantly in flux around one. This process strengthens the adult ego state.

In addition, having revisited my textbooks, I recognised the importance of using words to describe the experience one might have had, particularly if one is working within a group. So, it is not just hearing oneself use words that make the experience more meaningful; this dynamic also happens to those listening to the other members of the group. Their words are impactful.

I also began to think about sailing as a metaphor for living. Sailing is rich in metaphors, and the metaphor is an easy way of coming to understand complex, complicated ideas. To make sense of and to integrate an experience, a person needs to employ his or her ability to think, and the use of metaphor helps greatly in the process of transition from the conscious to the unconscious.

We started the next outing with participants from Bosence by making a simple therapeutic contract in the form of an outline of what each person would like to achieve from a day sailing. This may be something like learning about sailing, or improving self-confidence, or just having fun, or maybe all of these and a bit more. This was done within the group so that everyone could hear what each person wanted and could help each other achieve their goal. It also meant that I could tailor the activities to individual needs as well as the group's needs.

The other change I made to the programme was to put in place half an hour at the end of the day for reflecting and talking about how the day had been for each person. This was, to put it simply, a little bit of therapeutic group time, an opportunity to process and shape some meaning from the day's sailing.

As a result of one or both these changes I was pleased to find that I was being approached by members of the Bosence community several days after the event and being told about how the day had had a positive effect on them and what had been most beneficial. This opened the door for more communication and the opportunity to enquire a little deeper about how this had gone and what the positive effects were, and so the process continued. Crucially, getting off the boat, returning to the shore and back to Bosence was not the end of the process, it was just a part of it.

This was a highly fertile period for me, really thinking about what was going on onboard the boat and developing an understanding of what Adventure Therapy meant and how this could encourage the development of personal qualities and competences, and possibly affirming and strengthening existing ones. Sailing involves physical and psychological activities which carry a high perceived risk, but where the risk is in fact quite low. Consequently, the benefits for participants include having a positive experience of themselves and improvement of their self-concept, their resilience, resourcefulness and self-esteem. This word 'resilience' began to crop up more often; it was not something I had come across before, but I could recognise that my resilience had grown in recovery. It had developed, and I had become more capable of feeling, and coping with pain and happiness. When my resilience was low I couldn't bear pain for very long; I had to find an escape, but as my resilience grew I could contain myself for longer. This is a major shift in somebody's ability to process emotional difficulties, a major factor in the process of recovering from trauma and addictions.

The more I thought about it the more excited I became and realised I now had to take some detailed, practical steps. I had to get myself certificated and obtain a skipper's licence. This meant further sailing training to become an RYA Professional Skipper. Some have said that I was already certifiable but what I really needed was to get certificated. I also needed a licence to sail with paying clients. The first step was to get a Boatman's Licence, which was a legal obligation although it limited my sailing to within a line from St Anthony's Head at Falmouth to St. Nares Head at Helford. This meant I could sail three or four miles away from land and, most importantly, I could get insurance. The next step would be a Professional Skipper's Proficiency, which would allow me to sail 60 miles offshore.

So, I signed on for my skipper's sailing training. I had to demonstrate not just my sailing abilities but also learn new skills and techniques for sea survival, first aid, use of communication systems and electronics. My first effort was in spring 2002 and I didn't qualify. The next time I took it, in early autumn, when although conditions were rough, I passed all the tests and examinations. Although my log showed many hundreds of miles sailing, I had to demonstrate that I could calculate and describe what I was doing 'in the RYA way'; until then I tended to work out tides and driftage on my fingers. However, they now needed me to make specific calculations using a very particular method even if, when doing it my way, the results I had come up with were perfectly correct. This was frustrating and testing, as I didn't like having to do it their way, but I knuckled down and felt so much more confident and proficient on completion.

Learning to do this specific task in the prescribed and adult fashion was so contrary to how I had led my life while in active addiction. This process with the RYA was a metaphor for how I had grown up, and become a proficient, competent skipper and psychotherapist. I was making better choices based on real understanding of the here and now. I remember so well the difficulty I found in letting go of my old way of completing these tasks; I resisted, I felt irritated, angry and resentful and I could hear the voice in my head saying "F*** it! I know best...". I had to go through the whole process of letting go and asking for guidance; just a little isolated incident that summed up my whole recovery.

The next hurdle was to find some funding, and the gods were definitely on my side. I was advised of some limited European funding for those wanting to run trials prior to setting up a charity. This was perfect, and exactly what I wanted to do. I could run some more trials and hope to achieve tangible documented evidence of the experience, in order to create a charity. By being a legitimate charity, supported by the Charity Commission, Sailaday OK was more likely to be successful in its application for a variety of forms of funding that supported this sort of activity.

I had received some limited funding from the Cornwall and Devon Drug and Alcohol Agency to run small groups that summer in my boat *Serenade*. But now I was getting all my expenses paid and a little bit over to go in my pocket and help in the upkeep of the boat. However, to take myself seriously, I had to pay myself a realistic amount of money as a professional therapist and skipper, and to maintain the boat to a professional level. Initially, £2,000 of European funding was granted and I was so grateful. I think that, without this grant, we would have never got going.

The process of founding a charity was exhausting and frustrating. It was a detailed, specific process, and I needed the help of a solicitor to wade through the reams of questionnaires and directives. I had to put into words a mission statement, describing exactly how we were going to carry out this mission, and explain in detail how this would fit within the criteria set by the Charity Commission.

However, eventually, Sailaday OK was created. At this stage it consisted of myself, the solicitor, and a few friends and relatives who agreed to sign up as trustees. In order to fulfil the Charity Commission criteria, Sailaday OK required a number of trustees in specific roles: chairperson, treasurer, etc, but at this stage we just needed 'bums on seats.' However, we did have the makings of a true team, with a solicitor, an accountant, a man experienced in chartering and boating matters, a friend from the maritime arm of H M Customs and Excise, and a recovering addict.

The aim of the charity Sailaday OK was to reduce disadvantage and social exclusion by giving relief and rehabilitation to those recovering from addictions, abuse and trauma, through the provision of therapeutic sailing and marine-based therapies. So, it followed that I needed to define therapeutic sailing, and how it could give relief and rehabilitation to this client group, and where exactly all the participants were going to come from.

At this same time, my relationship with Bosence Farm was wearing a bit thin. I had been pushing for more supervision for myself and the other therapists, and I began to gain a reputation as a troublemaker. Nothing unusual there. Some of the others on the counselling team had no practical training at all; they were ex-residents and at the very least I thought they should have some supervision, but the management didn't seem to understand this necessity. I was becoming a nuisance and they looked for ways of getting rid of me, which was not an unfamiliar dynamic. Bosence Farm was a beautiful place, and a lot of the healing came through love and being in a place of tranquillity and peace. However, there was confusion, a serious rift in their identity; they considered themselves primarily as a 12-Step facility and not a Therapeutic Residential Centre. Whether they liked it or not, there were interventions and programmes with the residents that were therapeutic, so it *was* a therapeutic community. They were totally unclear about their boundaries and increasingly I had the feeling that this asylum was being run by the mad people.

This was a mistake I clearly didn't want to make with Sailaday OK; I needed to be absolutely clear that this was a therapeutic programme providing a challenging outdoor sporting activity as therapy. I was working on and exploring a unique therapeutic model to produce and promote positive personal change from practical experience. This was not about giving people a nice day out, and just hopefully doing them some good; it was a rigorous, experiential therapeutic process to bring about profound change.

I conducted some more one-day sessions with the residents from Bosence Farm and further trials with members of the 12-Step fellowships in Cornwall. I began to take some written feedback evaluations from these one-day sessions. These were simple evaluations, enquiring about their experiences and how the session might have been helpful for their recovery. There was also practical information about safety, provisioning and, most importantly, whether they would want to come again. One of the questions asked whether they wanted the session to be a lot longer, maybe several days. Over and over again the feedback was that one day was not enough; one daytime session was great but a programme of 24-hours or more would be a whole different ballgame.

In the autumn of 2003, I took *Serenade* out of the water for general upkeep and to prepare her for sale. I started looking for a more suitable boat to buy which I could then lease on a day-to-day basis to the charity. A larger boat would also mean that Sue and I could be a bit more adventurous in our sailing – heading off to France, Ireland and frequent visits to the Isles of Scilly. It is a wonderfully satisfying 12-hour sail to the Scilly Isles, involving some testing navigation and it is of course a stunning destination.

Around this time, I was making useful contacts in Plymouth who ran secondary long-term residential units. I met David, the manager of the secondary unit for men at Longreach and he was most interested in what we had been up to. He also recommended that I contact Wendy, the manager of the women's secondary residential unit in Plymouth.

At Longreach, people would receive primary treatment at one facility for 4 to 6 weeks. Then, if they wished to and they fitted the right criteria, they could go on to secondary treatment for an extended period of several months, with most staying for around 6 to 9 months. I felt that David and Wendy were both forward-looking and could immediately see the benefits of what I was planning and offering. Consequently, we started planning some trial sessions for the spring of 2004.

On New Year's Day 2004 I sailed a new boat back from near Chichester to Helford and my crew was one of the first participants to come out on a Sailaday OK session. He was in his early 20s, having had a life-threatening addiction to alcohol and had been homeless for the previous five years until he had arrived at Bosence Farm. He was so taken with the sailing that he decided that this was the life for him, and he signed up as a volunteer with outdoor education outfits in Cornwall who worked with young, disadvantaged people. He was then in the process of obtaining his certificates as an instructor of dinghy sailing, canoeing, and simple rock-climbing. He was our first success story, one of many to follow.

The new boat Sue and I bought we named *Physis*; the Greek word that describes a state of being both theological and philosophical and in English means 'nature'. The Greeks used this word to describe a natural energy, the energy of growth. This is the energy one might connect with, a self-actualising energy, when we sense the strong desire to move onwards and upwards. The drive to move towards one's highest desires and to move towards the light. So, *Physis* was an interesting metaphor for a boat which was driven forward by natural energies by a crew of people who are wishing for more in their lives.

5

Clean Bill of Health

*Clean bill of health: A certificate issued by a port
indicating that the ship carries no infectious diseases.*

"ATTACHMENTS, HATREDS AND hopes dissolve in the wake, dwindling until they seem far distant, as one faces the menacing and magical presence of the omnipresent sea, sorrow, desire, sentiment fades away, meaningless, because the ocean brings people back to themselves." Del Guado 1910[1]

The process of creating a new charity was frustrating and exhausting and took almost a year. Part of the problem was that the lawyer I employed didn't seem to know how to use emails and everything had to be done by snail mail. By the time we had gone through a few rounds of the process it was too late to jump ship.

I had found funding quite early in the process, making it possible to complete some of our early sea trials. This was funding from the European Union, and I will be forever grateful for their support, because at that time I was living on minimal income and would not have been able to finance these early trials or some of the early work involved in setting up the charity. Sailaday OK would not have been created at that time if it hadn't been for this European funding. Fortunately, though, within that time I was able to secure some funding dependent on complying with all the Charity Commission's requirements. Money came from the Big Lottery and a couple of local charities. I started to run groups with participants from Cornwall and Plymouth, using my own money, hoping to retrieve it later.

---

1   Spanish writer Arturo Perez-Reverte, Martin Cortes *Breve compendiode la esfera*; Jacques Dupuet; and Gabreil De Ciscar.

The trustees had little to do with the day-to-day running and managing of the charity. Their primary role was to oversee the charity, make sure all the 'i's were dotted and the 't's were crossed; also, that the business contract with me was watertight, that we were covered by insurance and the correct certification was in place.

It soon became clear that this project was really going to be a one-man band and, at that time, this suited me fine as I could just get on with what I wanted to do. However, later on this was to prove our Achilles' heel. It was a unique situation; my experiences and skills exactly fitted Sailaday OK, and its aims and ambitions were well suited to my skills and experience. I had been an active alcoholic and drug addict, with all that that meant socially, physically and emotionally. I had experienced recovery and was still working through that process and on a programme of recovery. I was also a confident and proficient sailing skipper; I had business skills and was a qualified and experienced psychotherapist. I had great empathy with the participants, I was emotionally connected, and I had the cerebral ability to think and develop the programme.

The first group from Plymouth was made up of three women, together with a member of staff to accompany them. This session was over two nights and basically went quite well except one night when we dragged our anchor as it was very stormy and windy. One of the participants got quite frightened and needed a lot of reassuring. My fear was that this incident would put people off, but it was quite the opposite; she was so pleased with herself that she had managed her fear well and taken support from the rest of the group. Even though there had been difficulties, the member of staff gave the thumbs up and the go-ahead to develop the programme; the next group was for four residents without a staff member.

It soon became clear to me that a two-day session was an inadequate amount of time. I remembered from my training that there were different stages in a therapeutic group process and Bruce Tuckerman described these as four stages of group dynamics.[2]

- **Forming:** orientating getting on with, and apparently getting along with others.
- **Storming:** letting the politeness down, letting your guard down a bit, finding fault and expressing more anger.

---

2 Therapeutic group process: Bruce Tuckman in 1965 described these as four stages of group dynamics – forming, storming, norming and performing, which is working in a group to a common goal. *Developmental Sequence in Small Groups.* Psychological Bulletin 63, 384-399.

- **Norming:** re-establishing the relationships with each other, developing trust and productivity.
- **Performing:** working as a group to a common goal and or helping each other to achieve individual goals, being cooperative and more efficient.

Two days would not give the group time to work through this dynamic. I made the decision to run groups for four days and nights. This was also about the limit of my capabilities and stamina and I suspected the limit for most boat virgins, remembering that I was taking them way out of their comfort zone and asking a great deal of them. There was also a huge amount on offer and much to absorb.

The next two groups, one with males and one with females, were far more successful and achieved the outcomes I was hoping for. The participants contributed to evaluation and feedback forms, recording their personal successes and achievements.

So, who were these people I was working with? On a superficial level, these were men and women recovering from addictions, abuse and trauma, and the primary aim was 'for the participants to have a positive experience of themselves'. An obvious and practical outcome would be that the experience would give them tools to help them in the completion of treatment and a longer-term outcome would be their re-integration into the community. The activities were structured, therapeutic, healthy, physical, educational, self-esteem enhancing and an enjoyable pursuit.

I promoted Sailaday OK so that the service was available to a marginalised and alienated element of society, who I believe from my own experience have a lot to give and have the potential to become valued members of the community at large. Statistical monitoring of the participants showed that most of our participants belonged to one or more of the following socially excluded groups: the unemployed, the homeless, ex-offenders and repeat offenders. In addition, the majority of those I worked with in the first sessions came from severely socially deprived neighbourhoods, in Cornwall or elsewhere in the UK. Typically, our participants were referred to us from NHS or third sector Drug and Alcohol Residential Centres. I needed to assess, using an intake process, whether they were at a stable stage of their recovery. Part of the assessment was to ascertain whether they would benefit from the Sailaday experience.

Sailaday OK had developed an innovative, effective and fulfilling therapeutic approach aimed at supporting the difficult process of transition from intensive residential drug and alcohol treatment centres to living in the community. The experience of a Sailaday session could be life-changing; it challenged participants in a supportive but intense way, to adopt new ways of viewing themselves and their relationships.

Completing treatment and having been on the Sailaday programme was a firm outcome, a box that could be ticked. However, most of the outcomes were 'soft': personal development, increased personal awareness, enhanced self-confidence and self-esteem. These are much harder to qualify and quantify and needed focus and some resolution when applying for funding. Our outcomes weren't to produce jobs, homes or training programmes, although these could well become by-products of people feeling more confident about themselves.

My experience and understanding of the essence of recovery is change, the ability to change and how to manage change. I was hopeful that this innovative programme would be a powerful catalyst for lasting change and consolidate the participants in their current stage of recovery and prepare them for re-integration and life back in the wider community.

From the very first moment they stepped aboard ship, they became aware that they were in an ever-shifting and changing environment. They had stepped out of their safety zone and were likely to feel some discomfort, a greater awareness of their environment, and their sense of the here and now.

There might have been early trauma in their lives or some specific events later in life, but all of them will have experienced physical trauma just by taking excessive amounts of drugs and alcohol to a point of becoming unconscious. I needed to be careful when working with such people as I was taking them into a risky environment. I didn't want to expose them to yet more trauma, which is the polar opposite of security. Learning how to manage an unstable environment, processing, sharing and normalising it with the help of the adult, the skipper, the main carer, and then eventually finding that they are safe and okay, is far more than just about survival; it is fertile ground for powerful healing.

I like this definition of trauma: "...any emotional response to life experience, whether of epic or apparently trivial proportions, which has not yet been processed."[3] (Parker Hall, 2008). Most traumatised clients we worked with had never developed the capacity to process their emotional experience, because in their early infancy "there [was] no one there" (Janet, 1907)[4] (Ilsley Clarke J & Dawson C) to help them regulate their effect. For

---

3   Parker Hall S, 2008, *Anger, Rage & Relationship: An Empathic Approach to Anger Management*, London, Routledge

4   Ilsley-Clarke J & Dawson C, 1998, *Growing Up Again: Parenting Ourselves, Parenting Our Children*, Minnesota, Hazelden

any number of reasons, their carer neglected, abused or was mis-attuned to them. "Traumatised people have not been protected in their early life and cannot protect themselves as adults. Until they enter therapy and there is someone there for them, they are vulnerable but also open to self-abuse and abuse by others." (Parker Hall, 2008).[5]

One of the obvious consequences of trauma is an inability to protect oneself as an adult. "Traumatised people are likely to have issues with boundaries and they are vulnerable to self-abuse/addictions, abuse of and by others. They are likely to have difficulty with intimacy and attuning to others." (Parker Hall 2008).[5] From my own experience, I understood that I could have quite a fragmented sense of self. Many I worked with on the boat were suffering dyslexia (non-genetic), and nearly all had some level of difficulty in learning and taking in (processing) new information – another consequence of trauma.

After the first eighteen months of processing evaluations, I was aware that many of these participants had other mental and psychological difficulties. More women than men suffered from dual diagnoses and reported mental illnesses. There was an almost equal split in those that had experienced family and domestic violence as well as attachment issues, and certainly more women than men had experienced childhood sexual abuse, but only by a few degrees. I was also to find that, within this client group, a higher percentage of women had issues around self-harm and eating addictions, although there were more men that suffered from other addictions such as work and gambling. There seemed to be an equal split amongst those suffering sex addictions.

I needed to add smoking, and a new one that was quite disruptive to all our groups: an addiction to mobile phones. These both required strong, clear boundaries to be set, and some people went to great lengths to try and break those boundaries. More than once I found somebody hiding in the toilet texting on their phone, and it wasn't unusual for this to be when we were sailing and preparing for a manoeuvre which called for teamwork and careful timing. If we were tacking, changing course, this needed to be done precisely and it was no good one of the team saying, "Hold on, just have to finish my fag and then I'll be with you", or "Somebody's texted me I must just answer". Grrr!

Many addicts have suffered physical and/or emotional abuse and consequently are significantly dissociated from their bodies; trusting their body is counterintuitive. In this maritime environment a participant's

---

5   2008, *Anger, Rage & Relationship: An Empathic Approach to Anger Management*, London, Routledge

impasse (Goulding M. and Goulding R. (1976)) "between embodiment and disembodiment, association and dissociation is heightened."[6] We were addressing this impasse at the heart of every Sailaday OK activity, and providing all necessary support, both formal and informal.

Participants were encouraged to connect with both their body and their surroundings, and the interventions, the exercises, sought to bring the participants as much into the present as possible, to experience the here and now. Through increased personal awareness, they learned to use the relationship with themselves to connect with the elements (or vice versa) and utilise their inherent wisdom and intelligence to better understand their current situation and what needed to be done – an obvious transferable skill.

For all this experience to have lasting benefit it needs to be processed and integrated. Exercises were debriefed and reflected on as they occurred. There was always a further opportunity to reflect upon the day's events in group 'process' time at the end of each day. Group members were encouraged to give and receive support to one another as they expressed their thoughts and feelings and to make personal meaning of these experiences for themselves. They were further invited to identify how learning and insights achieved aboard *Physis* could be transferred to their life ashore.

I knew from my own experiences and was encouraged when I could see this in the participants, how simple sailing activities had a therapeutic as well as a practical value. An activity like helming (steering) helps in this process of connecting.

Taking the helm, taking the wheel, being in control of the boat, is an activity that encourages the participant to use the body as an instrument to gather information about their environment. This intervention was carried out with the support of a therapist/skipper in close attendance and possibly with another member of the crew or peer. Group members were invited to trust all the sensory information that was available to them. When you attune and learn to use these sensory perceptions in this watery world around you, this is to achieve your goal, to get the boat from point A to point B safely and efficiently. Your sensory perceptions are:

- what you can see
- what you can feel through the motion of the boat (how she is moving, heeling etc)
- the feel of the wind and/or sun on the face, where it is hot and where it is cold

---

6   Goulding M & Goulding R. 1976; *Between Embodiment and Disembodiment, Association and Disassociation*

- the sound of the sails
- the feel and tension of the helm as you sense the rudder pressing against water

Participants incrementally increased awareness of their body and their relationship to the boat and hence to the environment. This led to a deepening of trust so they could then respond positively and usefully as they continued through the following progressive stages of helming – a fascinating interaction between the boat and the participant:

- By sight (towards a fixed point). Firstly, using a motor and then by sail.
- By compass (relying on sight and thinking). The helm needs to be manoeuvred counter-intuitively; this exercises the left-brain/right-brain activity, again firstly achieved using motor and then being driven by sail.
- By wind (relying on phenomenological responses). This is a more advanced exercise and I call it Zen sailing, where the sole object is to keep the wind at a particular angle. This isn't about getting from A to B.
- Blind helming. My Jedi Knights. Finally, this more advanced exercise was available, if it had been contracted for: an opportunity to do blind helming for 5, up to 30, minutes. Participants would work with a buddy, bringing in the elements of trust and cooperation. Trust all your senses and your guide. This was a more extreme exercise, teaching trust in your own phenomenological responses and your guide.

Each stage requires increased awareness of the present and a set of responses which resolve all problems to achieve one's goal. Participants make corrections to their course in response to environmental conditions. Each exercise calls for an increased awareness of the here and now. This is no time for letting one's mind wander into the past or future.

I will describe these exercises in more detail later in the book, as these exercises were developed further over the first few years. As well as practical sailing exercises, I used meditation and Tai Chi to help these people become even more aware, more in the here and now, more connected to their whole bodies.

Energetically speaking, a recovering addict tends to centre his or her energy around the upper chest and neck and higher; there is not much connection to the lower body. There is so much concern around being overwhelmed by emotions such as grief, fear and anger. However, a survival strategy can be learned in order to disconnect from the centres of this emotional energy where so much anger is stored: the heart, belly, around the navel, and lower. To successfully respond to the changes in the boat's movement and not keep falling over, one's centre of energy needs to be brought down to below the navel. So, exercises using Tai Chi bring the energy centres down lower in the body, helping participants to become more stable physically on the boat. A further consequence can be the achievement of more emotional receptiveness, but this requires careful monitoring and support where needed.

I often used simple yoga balancing exercises to help participants make these energetic changes within their bodies, to give them more stability and safety. Standing in a circle, on the bows holding hands, and then lifting one leg and balancing on one leg with the support of the others in the circle. This exercise is enhanced by letting go of each other and then, if people feel competent and confident enough, closing their eyes. At this point the boat would be anchored and moving in response to local conditions, wind, tide, passing boats; sea condition would need to be fairly stable.

I would be in attendance at all points and particularly observant of how they managed to walk or crawl or help each other up to the front of the boat and was always encouraged when I could see the difference in how they returned to the stern. They often would be walking more upright and just using the boat handholds to help them balance.

The meditation process I use is more akin to mindfulness practices, although when I started nobody was using the term 'mindfulness'. I have heard of other people using mindfulness on boats and have been quite shocked at their lack of empathy and knowledge of what the process is about. In one case, apparently, a participant was brought to tears when asked to go into stillness and quietness. This can give rise to highly negative emotions and memories, especially if suffering from trauma. I have also heard of people being told that they are "not doing it properly" or "not trying hard enough", shaming the participant and potentially creating more trauma. Certainly, in the early days, there was a lot of misunderstanding of mindfulness exercises and I do not consider them the 'be-all and end-all' that some people believe them to be.

I usually found that at least one person in every group I worked with was unable to sit quietly for five minutes, and certainly be unable to close their eyes without having some negative internal experience of themselves. It was too painful, and they could suffer from flashbacks. In these situations, I would try to normalise the experience by giving them some information about what might be going on. I would suggest that they might like to stay with the group, read or pray (if they were prayerful people), or sit quietly and mindfully suck on a mint, or if a smoker, have a cigarette. No shame, no pressure, but keep them included.

The meditation technique I use is to focus on one's breathing and then on some external stimulus. If sitting in the cockpit early in the morning, it may well be the sound of birds, water lapping or the wind. If the weather was unsuitable, we would sit inside the main cabin and just notice the sensations of movement as a body responds and flexes to all the gentle rocking movements of the boat. The purpose of these practices is to give people another way to experience the present moment exactly as it is – a reality check that is undeniable. This is how the present sounds, feels, tastes and smells – in some respects being mindless, not mindful. I encourage them to make no sense of what they are hearing or sensing as this is not a cerebral activity. This activity is one of being and discovering that the sensations and experiences are exactly how they are. This is the truth and the basis of our reality.

If the participant was really struggling, which many did, I would give them a Polo mint as this has a distinctive shape. Before eating the mint, I would ask them to feel it, look at the colour, shape and texture, and notice its size. To smell it, and really notice the smell, then put it in the mouth and move it around and again notice its taste and texture. Take one's time, focus, be aware that this is exactly as it is.

These sensations cannot lie to you; it's only what's in your head, your assumptions and beliefs about what is in your mouth that might be faulty. Your body cannot lie to you; it is only when you attempt to make meaning out of these sensations that your thinking can be faulty and consequently you make poor decisions.

6

Cut of His Jib

Cut of his jib: *The 'cut' of a sail refers to its shape. Since this would vary between ships, it could be used both to identify a familiar vessel at a distance, and to judge the possible sailing qualities of an unknown one. Sailors would recognise the nationality of other ships by the shape of the triangular foresail, giving rise to the modern use of the phrase: to judge the character of a person by the way they look — "I don't like the cut of his jib..."*

MAYBE IT IS time to listen to some of the feedback from participants from these first few years. The first two participants quoted below offered to write about themselves and how Sailaday OK had impacted upon them. I shall also be quoting feedback from other participants, male and female, giving their personal reflections on the experience from some of the feedback questionnaires sent out to residential centre management at that time. Also included is some of the 2010/12 Report Qualitative Evaluation undertaken by Dr Katherine Ashbullby.

Female, age 29

Presenting very emotionally withdrawn, although appearing very anxious. Intelligent and appeared to be using her intellect to hide behind. History of alcoholism and years of multiple substance abuse, and work addictions. (RH)

"There had been a lot of emotional abuse and violence in my early childhood. This was compounded by being the replacement child after the death of

my brother. It led to serious problems with identity, a tendency towards perfectionism and over-achieving. In other words, I was an alcoholic/addict waiting to happen.

I was traumatised further by an accident in the course of my "high flying" career which pushed me over the edge from "controlled" drinking to full blown alcoholism. My colleagues were killed overseas in a river accident while working on one of my projects. I was responsible for identifying the bodies, having them repatriated to the UK and dealing with bereaved relatives. There was also a lot of political fallout which was the most traumatising aspect of all. But I believe it was my inability to cope with the lack of having any control over their fate which actually brought me to my knees.

I had relapsed at a foreign embassy involved in the accident I mentioned above. It is a place full of memories and extreme pain. Unsurprisingly, I picked up a champagne glass instead of mineral water and two weeks later was back in a psych ward on suicide watch.... Then commenced a whole year spent mainly in hospital but interspersed with attempts at living at home during which time I could not cope with the extreme anxiety and drink again to make it go away.

The final episode was just after Christmas in 2010. I was admitted to hospital with bleeding from my stomach due to the quantities of alcohol which I had consumed. After another couple of weeks back yet again in the psych ward I was despatched down to Plymouth into treatment. I had very little motivation except for the thought that if there were the slightest glimmer of a chance that it might work; I had to give it a try. I was so anxious it felt as though my whole body was being invaded by some kind of alien life force. I was medicated up to the eyeballs. I was a barely functioning, tearful wreck....

Richard visited us in the early stages of treatment (at the residential) and when I heard what it (SOK) involved I felt sure I would not cope and made it emphatically clear that I would NOT be participating. However, I tried as much as possible in treatment to face my fears and found myself just deciding at the last minute to give it a go. It was hard in many ways. It was very different from anything I had done before and had a sense of myself as being devoid of all practical abilities. I also doubted I would handle being in such close quarters with the other women, who were not necessarily people I felt comfortable with back on dry land!

I realised though that there is something about being so far out of your comfort zone that makes it possible to connect with my real self. I became aware of my facades – my place of safety where I go when I cannot bear the fear and the pain. My place of safety is found in intellect and hiding in lots and lots of words. The others had their own places of safety and that might be very different to mine. Nevertheless, the feelings we were running from were the same. The sailing experience made it possible for the running to cease for a while, to give me a space to breathe, sense where the wind is, and where the sails are taking us. If we go off course, we have to take action to get back on course. We can of course influence our course but are at all times subject to the elements. I actually understood this on a spiritual level while at the helm one day. Perhaps this metaphor is enough of an understanding of my Higher Power, to what extent I am actually in control and where I need to accept the presence of greater forces than myself.

Overall, I learned a great deal in fact about acceptance in the course of my two sessions with Sailaday OK. Richard helped me to see that the real I, was not the intellectual keeping people and feelings at bay by erudition and force of words, but the woman who stood at the helm in the throes of massive anxiety but still holding her course.

I decided thereafter to accept my anxiety as being part of myself and palpably gave up the fight against it. Funnily enough when I started to practise this acceptance on a daily basis, the anxiety became manageable and started to subside. I know I will always be an anxious person, but these days the intensity has left me. I believe this not due to over ten year in the psychiatric system but due to what I learned on the two trips I did with Sailaday OK.

I am finally working though the AA programme after ten years of avoiding it and I am not so scared about facing the truth about myself and where my drinking has taken me. My mental health is much improved. I continue to be free from the crippling anxiety I had prior to going into treatment. I am not yet in paid work but love my voluntary job doing creative work with a bunch of homeless guys in a day centre in Kings Cross. I was tumbleweed like them. They are a creative, chaotic bunch so I fit in with them just nicely!

Above all, I know now that my firm convictions of things I am incapable of doing or indeed am not entitled to do are there to be challenged. I allow myself some optimism for the future. And whenever I get wound up and wired to the moon due to manic London life and I head for the South West where I can breathe again and reconnect my head to my heart." AH 2010

Female, age 33

Presenting very traumatised by childhood abuse and trauma and quite withdrawn, insular, anxious, depressed, bipolar. History of multiple drug abuse. (RH)

"Being raped by my father and death of sibling brother traumatised me. They have blamed me since and I blamed myself and dealt with this by drowning myself in drugs and alcohol and work. I have immersed myself in work and although held responsible positions, I have never seen myself as capable or able. All my relationships have been abusive and ended badly. I suffered from post-traumatic stress disorder, anxiety and depression.

The session with SOK was mixed. I found it very hard to get on with the other girls, always felt separate and different, couldn't join in the gossip and laughter. I loved the sailing and being really busy, didn't like downtime whether it was hot and sunny or raining, windy and had time out. I loved being at the helm and being in control.

I had also had very bad experiences on a boat with my father. I had intense feeling of unease and anxiety on the boat to start with and with a lot of love care and support from the skipper/therapist I began to separate him from my father, felt really powerful grief and anger, never allowed that before, bit of a shock. Now I feel this immense gratitude for life, I have always hated life and being alive, now I want to live and move on. Sailing is such a great metaphor for living, I am learning how to prepare for the journey and navigate the difficulties ahead. I really want to give myself a break and just go with the flow and not fight any longer, feel what I need to feel and take help where I can find it."

6 months later e-mail contact:

"I took your advice Richard; advice to do nothing much other than concentrate on my recovery, not to get into work and achieving again. Hard. But now

sometime later I am a different person, not driven, abstinent, love being part of the AA and NA culture and happier to be me. Looking forward to coming on one of the follow up sessions this year."

Returnee, being part of a RAT's group (Returnee Adventure Therapy) CW 2012.

The following is drawn from notes and reflections I wrote after the event with the following participants and includes texts from their evaluations.

Male age 46 from East London, of West Indian heritage

A long-term user of class A drugs, he had led a violent life as a blagger (bank robber), a drug dealer and pimp. Presenting as quite erratic, up one moment down the next. Possibly borderline, depressed and traumatised. Thoughtful and articulate, struggled with emotions. (RH)

His intake documentation included the following:

"I have spent most my life fighting for what I want. Violence and robbing being constants, so I really don't know how to live within the law, within normal community constraints, how to make a legal living. But I realised this time that I was going to die unless I changed, and I decided I want to live. But I aint got a clue how. My best mode of survival was to only trust myself and assume everybody was out to get something out of me, so strike first and bugger the consequences, it had to be better than letting anybody get close to me. I elected to Drug, Alcohol, and Substance abuse treatment." JW 2013

He found it hard on the boat, being confined to such a small area. He was a big guy, and he would say that the others in the group were good for a laugh and there was plenty to do during the day. Over the first few days he began to share a bit more about how it felt being part of a group and began to share his feelings, consequently he felt better about himself and he said he felt closer and more connected with the others.

The following event was recorded and filmed by the BBC South West team running a short news report:

He recounts the most remarkable experience when he was sitting in the cockpit during our lunch break enjoying the sun and the quiet and beauty of our surroundings. He felt calm he said and was enjoying just being there. He told me that he suddenly realised he felt content. When I enquired further about what was happening for him, he said he was absolutely amazed, he felt a complete transition, a complete change of his whole personality. He had never felt content or satisfied in his life, particularly from doing nothing. This seemed like an amazing breakthrough; a transitional insight that he hadn't got to do anything to feel good. This gave him permission to stop fighting; he could stop trying hard to achieve some happiness and peace. He recognised the enormity of this insight – that instead of striving and fighting all he had to do was nothing and just be responsive to feel satisfaction. He brought this insight to the evening group and received support from the rest of the team. More than that, the others could really recognise some similarities to their own experiences and said it was so good to hear somebody else expressing a sense of achievement and tranquillity and being okay by actually not doing very much at all. Hearing somebody else putting their experience into words helped them make sense of their own experiences – it was confirmation for all, and it gave them permission to feel good.

Female, age 28, Plymouth

Lifetime of drug abuse, alcohol abuse and physical abuse. Prostitution from the age 12.

Presenting inconsistent; willing to participate in all activities and thoughtful, very withdrawn emotionally and found it hard to express emotions. Symptoms of post-traumatic stress disorder.[1] (RH)

> In her words, *"I expected lots of high adrenaline sailing and being busy busy, 'cos that's what I'm like. I was anxious about the group time and didn't like talking about how I felt, I sort of go blank. But when the others shared what it felt like for them, I got really anxious, frightened and felt worthless. But Richard gave me a really good piece of advice to talk about the physical sensations, where in my body I was feeling whatever, and so slowly I could explore what was going on for me, it was like a door opening.*

---

1   PTSD: post-traumatic stress disorder. Mental, emotional disorder that can develop after a person is exposed to a traumatic event. This can develop after an apparently, trivial or a gross event. Those suffering from PTSD are at a high risk of suicide.

The sailing was slow and the weather hot so there was a lot of having to sit with me and I don't, correct, didn't like me. I believed in blotting out the past, "It's happened, can't change it so don't go there" but after one group where I shared my past and cried and a bit later, I realized I could look in the mirror and see me. I feel OK today, I don't ever remember when I could look in the mirror and feel OK about myself, today I did, thank you, and this will change my life, when can I come again?" NT 2014

Male, age 26, London

History of chronic drug abuse and alcohol abuse. Presenting depression, anxiety, symptoms of post-traumatic stress disorder. Learning difficulties as a consequence of trauma. Family issues and homeless.

"My big family won't have anything to do with me, I was always falling down drunk and they didn't drink at all, so I was the black sheep and lived on the streets and did whatever I had to do to get booze and get by. Nobody trusted me and I don't trust myself and I'm not surprised nobody trusts me after what I've done. When I was on the helm and you walked away and left me to it I was horrified, I'm going to f.... up, but I didn't and you must have known I was OK and I know now you were aware all the time what was happening, taking charge of the boat and being trusted has really changed me. Being trusted means I can learn trust myself more and start to trust others, I feel hopeful, I feel like all is possible..." MT 2014

Nearly everyone I came across had to overcome the monkey on their shoulder; the shadow of shame, and these were the sort of negative messages I would hear repeated over and over again – the voices of shame. These would be the underlying corrosive, toxic beliefs and misunderstandings of whom they thought they were:

"If you really knew what I was like, you'd hate me as well"

"If it wasn't for my wife, (job, parents, money, you) life would be fine."

"Nobody understands me."

"I never ever felt like I belong, whether it's with mates, family, even my children – they look at me as if I was a stranger."

"I don't trust nobody, they're only out for what they can get, what's in it for me anyway."

"I really think I'm a useless bit of s... everyone's always told me I'm stupid"

"I'm either god, invincible, and I can get away with anything or a waste of space, there isn't anything in-between."

Below is a summary of some of the findings from our qualitative evaluation report. These are the same people who described themselves so negatively above. Following four intensive days and nights there was often a massive change in attitude and beliefs.

Qualitative evaluation report 2010/12

Compiled by Dr Katherine Ashbullby, School of Psychology, University of Plymouth & European Centre for Environment and Human Health, University of Exeter Medical School.

The key findings can be summarised as follows:

- Participants enjoyed the experience and challenge of learning about and taking part in sailing tasks.
- Teamwork, social support and the opportunity to feel a sense of belonging and intimacy were a crucial part of what participants enjoyed about SAILADAY OK.
- The process group provided opportunities for participants to be honest about their feelings and emotions, and to receive and accept support.
- Richard was a key part of the trip for participants; participants reported Richard played an important role in helping them to have a positive experience and move forward in their recovery.
- Participants described improved feelings of self-confidence and self-worth following the trip.
- Participants also described feelings of calm and peace – for some this was related to the environment and being out at sea.
- A number of participants enjoyed the beauty of the scenery during the sailing and described the ocean as providing freedom and a sense of peace.

- For others sailing led to positive emotions, but these were excitement and a sense of adventure from the challenges of sailing.
- Participants liked the fact that the experiences and skills they gained during sailing could be applied to help them with their recovery. The process group was important in allowing participants to recognize and reflect how sailing related to their recovery process.
- Participants could recognise the positive change in their attitude about themselves.
- Participants spoke about having had a spiritual experience and feelings of gratitude.
- Participants reported the experience had opened their eyes to a new way of life and it left them feeling more confident and refreshed, with hope for the future.
- Participants did experience challenges and difficulties during the trip related to the confinement, shared sleeping space, and lack of privacy, difficulty sailing in rough weather, sick sickness, and negative emotions.

7

By and Large

By and large: *By means into the wind, while large means with the wind. "By and large" is used to indicate all possible situations − "The ship handles well both by and large".*

I BELIEVE THAT when Sailaday OK combined an empathic psychotherapeutic relationship with sailing, this dynamic created the optimum environment to stimulate the individuals' latent organismic capacity (their Physis). The Greek word Physis, now the name of our yacht, describes our natural energy that when we connect with it, we are lifted towards our higher consciousness. We are then more likely to regulate and process not only our here−and−now emotional experiences, but also any archaic experience which may surface during the process. This led me, in 2008, to co−write (with Sue Parker Hall) an article which was published by the International Stress Management Association and appeared in the journal *Addiction Today,*[1] one of the outcomes of which was an invitation to make a presentation to the 6th International Adventure Therapy Conference (IAT) in Edinburgh in 2010.

This was a very productive period for me, preparing my presentation at Edinburgh, as well as managing the groups and developing our programme at sea. I had tended to be instinctive and rely on my intuition when integrating therapy theory. However, now I had to think about what was happening on the boat, clarify the theory, explain the process, and write it down. This was not something that came easily to me and I was greatly helped and supported by Sue. Writing a presentation for peers is a very different matter to completing funding application forms, and I had to negotiate a steep

---

1 Lannowe Hall R & Parker Hall S 2008, *Addiction Today*, Analysis of a marine wilderness therapeutic activity.

learning curve. Similar to when I had to learn how to sail the RYA way, I had to use my left brain to make sense of what my right brain intuitively understood, and then back this up with references and other established theories. This helped me to clarify my theoretical understanding of Sailaday OK's process, in that we were using sailing as a therapeutic tool.

I worked with those who had been in recovery long enough to achieve some behavioural changes and who were, at the time, confronting the developmental and life traumas that were at the root of their addiction. Clients confronting these difficulties experienced the intolerable feelings and negative self-beliefs that they had previously managed with their addiction but could now no longer avoid.

Through qualitative and quantitative therapy outcome research, SOK developed an empirical integrated therapeutic model. As you can read from some of the feedback, we generally found that clients experienced lasting positive changes. Facilitating an effective therapeutic relationship was at the heart of SOK's approach. In addition to psychotherapy theory and practice, we used experiential education, adventure therapy and ecotherapy theories and methods to help us to strengthen our relationship alliance, enabling us to understand clients' processes, increase the effectiveness of our interventions and communicate our approach to clients, referrers, funders and peers.

From my own personal experience, my knowledge of addictions and the behaviour that is demonstrated while in the throes of addiction, I clearly understood that this is just a visible symptom of an underlying disturbance. Addictions and other traumas are broad and complex issues, but SOK had chosen to focus on the process of change that is necessary for successful recovery; our interventions targeted clients' behaviour, cognition, and emotional responses to strengthen their capacity to change.

Clients were supported to:

- accept and consolidate their present stage of recovery
- develop and/or strengthen their ability to adapt in a healthy way to the ever-changing circumstances of sailing/life in the here-and-now
- process historical negative experiences and beliefs that prevent change
- prepare themselves for re-integration into the wider community

Over this period of practice, reflection, re-evaluation and consultation, SOK had created a unique, integrated therapeutic understanding of recovery from addiction, trauma and the consequences of abuse. We had

69

developed a methodology which enabled us to measure, communicate and make sense of the changes the clients were making when participating in outdoor experiential education or adventure therapy. Intervening with maximum impact at the right time at the right moment facilitated positive changes. This process incorporated, and was underpinned by, the following approaches:

- Transactional Analysis (Berne)
- Neuroscience (Schore) and Eye Movement Desensitisation Reprogramming (EMDR) (Shapiro)
- Developmental theory (Ilsley-Clarke and Dawson)
- Applied Jungian and Relational Analysts' theory
- Experiential Education
- Carl Rogers and Client-centred therapy
- Adventure and Ecotherapy
- Mindfulness

All the above are referred to in more detail in the references.

Transactional Analysis has useful assessment tools and models including the Parent, Adult & Child, the Karpman Drama Triangle and OK Corral models.[2]

Lasting change is understood to be facilitated by the 'integrating Adult ego state' described as "a set of feelings, attitudes and behaviours that are present-centred [and] integrating... not controlled by past influences and experiences."[3] (Summers & Tudor, 2000)

The majority of SOK's sailing and therapeutic exercises were designed to help clients to connect with their Adult ego state in order to be able to orientate themselves in their immediate environment but also to process any inhibiting Parent ego state messages or archaic Child ego state experiences which may be triggered.

SOK had a psycho-educational component. Clients further deepened their understanding of the nature and consequences of addiction and trauma. In particular, they learned how people who are traumatised are not only unable to process the experience which afflicted them in the first place but frequently have been unable to process many subsequent life events,

---

2   Karpman, Drama Triangle and OK Corral models: Kartman defined the Drama Triangle as a social model of human interaction in 1968. The Triangle maps a type of destructive interaction that can occur among people in conflict. The Drama Triangle model is a tool used in psychotherapy and specifically in transactional analysis. The main actors are the victim, the rescuer and the persecutor.

3   Integrated adult ego state: see Berne (Summers & Tudor, 2000).

resulting in a multiple pile-up of emotional experience until they can develop their Adult ego state and start to differentiate and process.

Underlying issues of trauma and shame

Trauma: Defined as "any emotional response to life experience, whether of epic or apparently trivial proportions, which has not yet been processed."[4]

Some consequences of trauma:

- Inability to protect themselves as adults. Issues of boundaries and are vulnerable to self-abuse/addictions and abuse by others and abuse others. (Parker Hall, 2008)
- Mis-attuned to others and have intimacy difficulties
- Have a fragmented sense of self
- Likely to suffer dyslexia (nongenetic)
- Difficulty in learning and taking in (processing) new information
- Understanding and knowledge about shame and rage, normalising

Session after session, I found I was working with the participants' difficulties in coming to terms with these underlying issues. There was not a lot of time spent talking about drugs and alcohol and associated cravings. But there were opportunities made for them to recognise how trauma had created the right environment for them to use addictions to help to control the consequences of trauma.

Again and again, I would listen to individuals expressing their loathing of themselves and talking about the dark black hole they were inhabiting. When offered an opportunity to describe it they would talk about the lack of light, the fear of letting anybody see this part of themselves. They would say things like, *"I am not normal, I will do anything not to let anybody see this part of me"*, and when we managed to name this shame and give it some normality and reality there was always a great feeling of relief and grief, and sometimes anger.

The act of naming and recognising that they had been traumatised and that they were experiencing shame seemed to open doors for them. Even though it might be frightening, if they had the resilience to take the risk and

---

4   Parker Hall S. 2008 *Anger Rage and Relationship; and an empathic approach to anger management*, London Routledge.

stay vulnerable, then they might have the opportunity to walk through into the light.

Shame: Defined as, "An emotionally and sometimes physically painful affective state caused by the initial impact of any kind of pre-conception, pre-natal or postnatal experience of an environment that is hostile or failing (trauma); experienced personally as a 'fall from grace'. Ruptures the relationship with self, others and the wider environment."[5]

Neuroscience and EMDR[6]

We know from neuroscience that, to process trauma, both left and right brain need to be engaged at the same time.[7] **EMDR** (Shapiro, 1989, 2012) uses bilateral stimulation (eye movement or taps) because what Shapiro discovered was that the heart of the therapy is that you cannot *not* process whatever material you are focusing on when both right brain and left brain are being stimulated at the same time.

But bilateral stimulation can happen in other ways. For example, through experiencing an empathic relationship which encourages the processing of emotion through using left brain language to express right brain experience. This is at the heart of psychotherapy.

Bilateral stimulation also occurs when sailing, just by being in a state of heightened awareness. For example, steering and using a compass often involves behaving counter-intuitively, and performing any task aboard, from making tea to using the toilet and maintaining balance, you need to think and feel at the same time. This will stimulate healing and internal change.

---

5   Parker Hall, S, 2014, *Understanding and Healing from Shame, handout, Working with Shame* workshop.

6   Neuroscience and EMDR (Shapiro): "EMDR, Eye Movement Desensitisation and Reprocessing, is a form of psychotherapy developed by Francine Shapiro in 1988." The World Health Organisation wrote this guideline but EMDR is based on the idea that negative thoughts, feelings and behaviour are the result of unprocessed memories. American Psychological Association lists EMDR as an evidence-based treatment for PTSD.

7   The majority of traumatised clients we work with have never developed the capacity to process their emotional experience because in their early infancy. "There [was] no one there". Janet, P, 1907, *The Major Symptoms of Hysteria*, London and New York, MacMillan. Their carer neglected, abused or was mis-attuned to them. It is likely those suffering from trauma at an early age may well have deficits in there early developmental stages. Sailaday OK addresses these areas.

Developmental theory[8]

Most of the traumatised clients we work with have never developed the capacity to process their emotional experience because in their early infancy "there [was] no one there" (Janet, 1907). Their carer neglected, abused or was misattuned to them. It is likely that those suffering from trauma at an early age may well have deficits in there early developmental stages, and Sailaday OK addressed these areas:

BEING (infancy): Expanding of self-awareness to all sensations and being in the world. The existential question being asked is, "Can I trust the world?"

DOING (toddlerhood): Participating in the experience, an existential recognition that I am I and you are you.

THINKING (2-4yrs old): Processing and making sense of the experience. The existential question being, "Is it okay to be me?"

- **Being:** Creative, reflective, passive, allowing feeling/sensational
- **Doing:** Pro-active, play, explore, risk-taking, experiential
- **Thinking:** Reflect, make meaning, be mindful, measure, evaluating, use words

Being

By being and finding a state of heightened awareness. Steering and using a compass often involves behaving counter-intuitively, and when performing any task aboard you are in a world of feelings and sensations. Moving around on board requires a new awareness as you need to engage with your body. This will stimulate healing and internal change.

Doing

"By doing we learn experientially" (Jung)

Increase resilience and we develop our sense of self, and our vitality. Resilience is a new word in my vocabulary. After going to Edinburgh, I

---

8   Developmental theory: developmental psychology generally focuses on how and why certain changes (cognitive, social, intellectual and personality) in the course of the human life occur over time. Eric Erickson developed a model of eight stages.

realised it was something I had been working with unconsciously, but now I could consciously incorporate this really important element into our programme. Although sailing with a qualified skipper is mostly fairly low-risk, for the inexperienced it can feel quite high-risk. Risk and risk-taking is an important element of outdoor/adventure/eco therapies in the development of resilience.

- "The right amount of risk and responsibility helps children and teens become resilient" (Michael Unger)[9]
- Resilience does not eliminate or decrease the pain; rather, it permits intolerable discomfort to be accepted and 'owned'
- Resilience helps us to develop our capacity to navigate our needs (having what you need made available and accessible)
- The capacity to negotiate (and influence what is provided)[10]

Thinking

To make sense of and to integrate an experience, you need to employ your ability to think, and the use of metaphor is the bridge. Metaphors help to make the transition from conscious to unconscious. (See Chapter 11)

Client-centred therapy[11]

Carl Rogers proposed that therapy could be simple, warm and optimistic: "The individual has within himself or herself vast resources for self-understanding, for altering his or her self-concept, attitudes and self-directed behaviour – and that these resources can be tapped if only a definable climate of facilitative psychological attitudes can be provided".

Client-centred therapy[12] operates according to three basic principles that reflect the attitude of the therapist to the client:

---

9   (Michael Unger) *You Resilience and Culture*, NY ISBN978-04-017-9414-5
10 The capacity to negotiate (and influence what is provided) (S. Levine, Poesis 1992)
11 Client-centred therapy; Irvin D Houghton Mifflin, I Kaplan and Carl Rogers are American psychologists and the founders of the humanistic approach of the person-centred way of understanding personality and human relationships. Rogers CR, 1980, *A Way of Being*, Mariner Books.
12 *Client-centred approach; client centred therapy* 1951 London Constable; Rennie DL, 1998, *Person-centred counselling: an experiential approach*, London, Sage.

- The therapist is **congruent** with the client
- The therapist provides the client with **unconditional positive regard**
- The therapist shows **empathetic** understanding to the client

These three principles are the basis for creating a favourable therapeutic relationship for the process of change to take place. In my private practice I learned to develop this relational approach and it is completely consistent with my beliefs that to 'hold' the client at this difficult time of change is beyond the therapeutic and feels more like a spiritual process.

Sailaday Formal Group Process Time

This was a one-hour confidential time for a group process at the end of each day. I came to understand that this was a most important element of our process, where experience could become integrated and embedded. In this way, the experiences clients may have had with Sailaday could help them to resolve difficulties back ashore. Without this time to process and integrate, the learning that may have taken place could dissipate quickly. The benefit of having time to think and put the experience into words allowed the experience to filter through and become integrated with their life ashore. The ability to support the participant in this difficult and painful process of turning a jolly day's sailing into a therapeutic and positive process of change is what made Sailaday unique. I have often heard the criticism that these people would need to go sailing all the time to be able to resolve their difficulties in living successfully ashore, and to feel okay about themselves. My own personal experiences and the feedback from our participants proved this not to be the case.

Group time was confidential and became time to:

- reflect
- feed back
- process, share, talk about the day or what might have been triggered during the day
- process group dynamics and or conflict
- give information where needed i.e. definitions of trauma and shame
- encourage thinking and the use of metaphors to explain difficult ideas and support transition
- encourage feeling

- confront denial and negative beliefs
- process stages of group development, forming, storming, norming, and working
- encourage to attend to the process, and not the content or outcomes.

My time in Edinburgh was quite amazing. I loved it and found it quite challenging, being amongst so many knowledgeable people from all over the world who are practising outdoor education and adventure therapy.

I hope I didn't come across as naïve, but I had no idea that this sort of work was happening out there all over the world. I had felt as if I was in a bubble and had come to believe that nobody else was creating anything like my work with Sailaday OK. My presentations and workshops were received extremely well, and people were impressed and expressed active interest. Firstly, in the uniqueness of working at sea with a therapeutic residential programme, but also with our reported outcomes.

My only disappointment in Edinburgh was that I found nobody else to compare notes with about the maritime experience. However, there were many similarities with those that trekked mountainous deserts and wildernesses. The woman I felt most inspired by works in Gaza in Palestine, with highly traumatised young people. *Adventure Landscape* was a courtyard with a lemon tree in it. Often suffering from stray bullets and shrapnel, the children would experience childhood with the help of a lemon tree. She was inspirational and I came to understand that you don't need a vast landscape or seascape, you just need the right trigger and an empathic relationship to explore the trauma.

As well as learning a huge amount about the history of experiential education and adventure therapy, I also discovered new words that I quickly embraced and they became part of our programme: risk assessment, risk benefits, wellbeing,[13] and resilience. Resilience was something that had developed in my recovery, and I could clearly see how I could achieve the capacity to contain, and eventually process, the pain and distress that was eating me up: the feelings of inadequacy, rage, trauma and shame. It meant I could take the risk of feeling them longer and deeper until a process of transformation took place.

Wellbeing was a term I hadn't come across before. I came to understand it as an inclusive term and a way of measuring our emotional, physical, spiritual and cultural health. I realised that this was part of the jigsaw, a way

---

13 Wellbeing: Signifying a wellness and a condition of an individual group and may include their physical vitality and mental alacrity, social satisfaction, spiritual awareness, a sense of personal fulfilment and accomplishment and cultural satisfaction. (RH 2000)

of evaluating progress and positive change. This was going to help greatly in our funding applications if I could measure and assess the improvements in somebody's wellbeing. When there is positive change, one becomes more stable, more sure of oneself. Here is evidence of the rock that the person can stand on so that they can become a more functioning and positive member of the community. This was a task I needed to undertake as soon as I got home, but I needed help to develop a process of evaluating the changes in the participant's wellbeing.

I hadn't realised how much research had gone into understanding the benefits of being in the green environment, which also helped me understand the area I was working in – the blue environment. This was another door opened for me to undertake more reading and research on my own account. Some of the research benefits I heard about at the Edinburgh event are listed below.

Researched benefits of being in the green environment:[14]

- Green play settings benefit children with ADD/ADHD (Taylor, Kuo & Sullivan)
- Outdoor activity reduces myopia (Rose, et al)
- Children living on streets with trees have less asthma (Lovasi, et al)
- Green exercise reduces blood pressure and improves mood (Preety et al)
- Nature buffers life stress amongst children (Wells & Evans)
- Views of nature improve recovery from surgery (Ulrich)
- Increased sense of wellbeing when there is a reduction in noise and pollution or in a green environment (NHS)
- Life expectancy is related to presence of natural landscapes (Poudayl, Hodges, Bowker, & Cordell 2009)
- Long term improvement in overall health, faster physical recovery from illness, stress, and trauma (NHS)

It was all a considerable learning curve for me, and I learned that adventure therapy is a distinct and separate form of psychotherapy which had become prominent since the 1960s. Influences from a variety of learning

---

14 There are a variety of studies to explore; Green play settings benefit children with ADD/ADHD (Taylor, Kuo & Sullivan); Outdoor activity reduces myopia (Rose, et al.) Green exercise reduces blood pressure and improves mood (Preety et al.); Nature buffers life stress amongst children (Wells & Evans); Views of nature improve recovery from surgery (Ulrich); Increase sense of wellbeing when there is a reduction in noise and pollution or in a green environment. (NHS); Life expectancy is related to presence of natural landscapes (Poudayl, Hodges, Bowker, & Cordell,2009); Long term improvement in overall health, faster physical recovery from illness, stress, and trauma. (NHS)

and psychological theories have contributed to a complex theoretical combination now known as Adventure Therapy (AT). The roots of this can be found in proponents of experiential education; for example, The Guides and Duke of Edinburgh's Award[15] and other similar programmes and even earlier theories developed by the relational analysts which includes Jung. Jung came to the conclusion from the study of Eastern and Western philosophies and psychology that "It is likely that we cannot understand a thing until we have experienced it inwardly." (Jung)

Relational analysts believe "experience is the foundation for internal change".[16] This idea is a cornerstone for the thinking behind the development of experiential education and helped me to make sense of what I had been doing intuitively.

I realised that I had taken for granted my connection and relationship with nature and particularly what the marine and watery element of nature meant to me and had spent no time analysing it and putting it into words. In Edinburgh, I came to understand that there was a common theme – the need to re-connect with nature, recognising the multiple benefits of the varying ways this can be done. The early use of adventure therapy was to take from nature and benefit from it. However, there seemed to be a lack of awareness of the need for a more eco therapeutic relationship. Eco Therapy is not opportunistic – it creates a three-way relationship between the client, the therapist and the environment. Key elements found in AT that differentiate it from, or link it to, other therapeutic approaches integrated into this definition include:

- The positive influence of nature in the therapeutic healing process through the use of eustress or the positive use of stress.
- The active and direct use of client participation and responsibility in their therapeutic process.
- The involvement in adventure experiences meaningful for the specific client, particularly in terms of natural consequences.
- The focus on positive changes in the client's present and future functional behaviour.

---

15 Duke of Edinburgh's Award: introduced in 1956 by Prince Philip, the Duke of Edinburgh, there were three levels – bronze, silver and gold, and participants were asked to set certain objectives including, community volunteering, physical activity practical skills, expedition planning and adventurous journeys. These may include some residential time taking part in these activities.

16 Guides and Scouts: This is a non-political educational movement for young people which originated in the UK by Lord Baden Powell. Although developed a hierarchy of Brownies Guides and Scouts, the programme was an informal educational setting with the emphasis on practical outdoor activities. Many from urban backgrounds had the opportunity to spend time in the natural environment.

- The strong ethic of care and support embraced throughout the therapeutic experience.

Most of this I had been doing instinctively and Sailaday OK seemed to be bordering on eco and wilderness therapy, possibly moving away from the more opportunistic adventure therapy.

I was finding that participants became more aware that they are part of a greater ecosystem and are not as bound by social customs and norms. In essence, participants can be true to themselves and more able to see others as people, regardless of race, class, religion etc. Outdoor education also helps instil the basic elements of teamwork because participants often need to work together and rely on others. For many people the intensity and intimacy of being aboard a smallish boat may stretch their levels of comfort zone and cause them to challenge themselves physically which, in turn, can lead to challenging oneself mentally, emotionally, relationally and spiritually.

The use of adventure as part of a healing process can be traced back in history to many cultures. We were doing this thousands of years ago; today all that has changed is our condition. Leaders, wise men/women were taking people out into the forests to meet their 'Demons' and be healed thousands of years ago. Here in Cornwall, there is evidence of just such practices. There is evidence that this took place, not only in Britain, but also among native Americans, in Africa, and in Jewish and Christian traditions, and most tribal cultures.

Process of transition

A rite of passage; again, this was something I had incorporated into our programme unconsciously and, I guess, quite instinctively. Sailaday's process incorporated this rite of passage: leaving, immersion, returning, and celebration. As well as a new understanding through my research I had found that, here, in the heart of Cornwall, was ancient knowledge and an understanding that I could build upon and develop with Sailaday OK.

8

To Let the Cat Out of the Bag

To let the cat out of the bag: The punishment for the most serious misdemeanours in the Royal Navy was flogging. This was administered using a whip called the 'cat o' nine tails'. The cat was kept in a leather bag.

IT NEVER CEASES to amaze me when, after all the efforts made to give participants the experience I think they need, events unravel all my best intentions. However hard I try to get it right, nature throws me a wobbly, which often can be irritating, disconcerting, disorientating and darn right bloody-minded. Even so, on reflection, and when I work through the process, it is nearly always positive and helpful.

This is exactly what happened one day in midsummer on the third day of our residential session with a group of women. I had a plan for the day which was carefully crafted to support the events and activities from the day before and to help the women create some more that day.

I woke up to find that the electricity had drained from the batteries during the night, making it impossible to start the engine and there were no lights or other essential services needing power. We were marooned, anchored near St Mawes about 3 miles from Falmouth harbour – about half an hour away if we were to motor. However, we had no motor and we had practically no wind. It was a beautiful blue-on-blue sunny summer's day.

We were aboard a sailing boat and so we had to *sail* into the harbour and find a point on the Falmouth Haven pontoon, where we could tie up and plug in to recharge our batteries. Sounds easy enough, on a day with a reasonably helpful wind, which is not what we had that day. To add to that it was a summer's day and there were quite a number of other boats about.

To get anywhere near the pontoon was a delicate sailing operation and, to get the best of the wind and to avoid bumping into anybody else, we had to make several tacking and course changes. It took us about 6 hours! With a skilled crew this would still have called for demanding seamanship, but we did not have the luxury of a skilled and experienced crew.

As we came across the harbour, we readied the boat for landing, put out the fenders, prepared all the necessary bits of rope to tie up fore and aft and our spring lines amidships. I briefed the crew as to what was expected of each of them and, in particular, the one who was going to stand on the bows and take the bow line ashore as soon as she could stretch and jump that far and secure us to a bollard.

The crew member elected to do this task was called Amber; she was enthusiastic and keen to help – although probably not the fittest person, but very willing and eager to please. She had always been a vocal and vibrant member of the group, had a big personality and was generally big in every other way.

As we got nearer to the pontoon, I spied a small gap between two other boats that I hoped we could slide into. It took several attempts to get the angle right and the process clear in everybody's minds. As we got closer, the sails needed to be dropped and the two people, one on the stern and one on the bows, ready to go ashore with the ropes, jumping at the right moment when given the word. Each time we failed to get the angle right we had to sail back out and tack around in quite a big circle, avoiding many other boats that were moored in the area. This was getting more and more difficult and the tension was rising.

Finally, we got the angle, and we were drifting into position, but then we hit a snag that wasn't quite what I expected. As we got nearer to the pontoon, within a few yards, we created a cushion of air between us (the yacht) and the pontoon. The consequence of this was that we were pushed back out again away from the pontoon. Each time we got to the spot, Amber was getting more and more vocal and excited and I expect quite nervous as she had to step across the gap or jump – her role was vital. I was getting exasperated and beginning to feel somewhat negative and looking for another solution to our problem. Amber was also clearly getting emotional and stressed.

One last try and one more time we came to within a few yards and then halted. At that very moment, an elderly man in a tiny inflatable dinghy was motoring past us. I hailed him and asked him to give us some help. He did better than that, gently turning his dinghy towards our yacht, which was a great deal larger than his little dinghy, and he gave us the tiniest of nudges, a little help to push us in the right direction. There was no big drama, he just gave us the slightest of pushes and we swept in alongside the pontoon. Absolutely perfect, a beautiful landing, everyone did their job, a little bit of stumbling and dropping of ropes but in the end, all was good and, by the time I turned round to thank the man, he was long gone.

By then, Amber was standing on the pontoon looking very pleased with herself, hysterically shouting, laughing and gesturing. I thought that something must be wrong – maybe she had dropped the rope or something – but she was just highly excited and doing what she did best, making a huge drama out of a small event. She had everybody's attention including crews from the neighbouring boats.

Next step was to plug in our mains line to get power up, put on the kettle and review our situation. Amber joined us in the main cabin, still being quite vocal, and I began to get the drift of what she was saying. She was repeating over and over, *"It was just a tiny little boat that gave us a tiny little push that made all the difference to our great big boat"*. We all just said... *"Yes Amber, you are quite right"*, not quite sure what else to say really. I certainly hadn't quite grasped the significance of what she was saying and why this was so meaningful for her.

It was now time for a late lunch, a little siesta and then off back out to sea to find somewhere quiet and safe to anchor for the night. It was later on, in group process time after dinner, that she began to make a bit more sense of her experience. She explained to us that all her life she had felt that she needed to make a big noise, big dramas, to get what she wanted. This had often led her to behave in ways that got more attention than she really wanted, particularly with men. She had attracted abusive and violent people who revelled in the dramas she created. The more abusive they became the more extreme her behaviour. It was a vicious cycle and her need to please had driven her into dangerous situations.

One of the conclusions she had come to recently had been that she never really got what she wanted and certainly never got what she really needed, which was to be liked and loved for just who she was. Of course, the difficulty was that she was so used to behaving outrageously that she had forgotten how to be just herself. She had also reached the conclusion that her size had reflected this need to be big, to be seen as 'more than'.

I marvelled at how the rest of the group came around and supported her, giving her the really good feedback that they liked her better when she was quieter and behaving more reasonably. She admitted that this was hard to understand, and just didn't make sense to her.

There was a moment during this group time that she became quite quiet and was clearly lost for words. We gave her time and space to be exactly how she was, and I reminded her that it was "fine just to be quiet". With this permission, the tears flowed and she began to express the grief she felt about having wasted so much time behaving as she had. She felt so sad and grief-stricken that she had lost something essential that she couldn't quite put a finger on. She said, *"I feel as if this big bulk of my body has been hiding the essential me. Nobody else can see me, nobody can see me and I can't see me"*. This all felt very real to me, as this was her real self talking about the parts that had been lost. I felt a lot of love for her.

She then got to a stage where she wanted to retreat, and told us that she was, *"Fine, and I'm okay..."*, but I needed to pursue this a little bit further as I wanted her to make a decision. She contracted to stay in the group and not run away, and I asked if there were some changes she would like to make now. There was a moment's quiet before the dam burst and she said really clearly, *"I never have to behave like that again. That little boat nudging the big boat, so it got exactly what it wanted and needed was how I could now be. I can ask for what I want and keep it all in proportion, God what a relief"*. She was smiling and crying and laughing and so was everyone else.

I kept in touch with this person for several years afterwards. Although she had many difficulties to overcome and had some behavioural relapses, she always treasured that moment, and would often tell me that it had been the turning point in her life, and nothing was ever the same again.

I felt very humble and grateful that day. Something quite marvellous had happened and it had been quite beyond my control. However hard I tried I could never have arranged the situation when a person or group can be given an opportunity to change their lives and they grab it with both hands. This truly is what is meant by being in the right place at the right time – all you need to do is turn up and be open, honest and willing.

I taught everyone who came on the boat this truth. For example, you cannot control what is happening on the boat when you are on the helm and skippering – you can only work with what you are given. To emphasise this, I explain that helming a boat is an art form; it is not about control, as there is no such thing as a perfect helmsperson. You need to learn, to get out of the way, feel the impact on your ego, feel the powerlessness and trust the process. We cannot control the weather, nor can we control other people. We only have personal choices and sometimes the best we can do is just turn up. Amber had no idea that day that those events were going to change her life and they wouldn't have done if she hadn't been committed to the process and been willing and prepared to be supported. When participants experience such things while on the boat, it is clearly not just about sailing. This is what they have to integrate into their lives, and many did. They could then maintain their course and achieve success by working with what they have been given.

9

Over-reaching

Over-reaching: When tacking, holding a course too long.

"Even when it's dark, I don't have to be lost"[1] (RH 2012)

ADVENTURE THERAPY ENCOURAGES the development of new personal qualities and competencies whilst affirming and strengthening existing ones; it involves physical and psychological activities which carry a high perceived risk but where the actual risk is low. The benefits to participants include having a positive experience of themselves and improving their self-concept, sense of resilience, resourcefulness and self-esteem.

Sailaday OK integrated the healing potential of the natural environment and psychotherapy to provide an experiential learning opportunity that supported recovery from addiction, abuse and other forms of trauma. My work was underpinned by the notion of sailing as a metaphor for recovery. Both require a high degree of awareness of the surroundings and personal resourcefulness to navigate the ever-changing conditions. Sailing offers concrete experiences which, when debriefed and processed, deliver learning that can easily be transferred to the recovery process.

Alcohol and substance addictions are conceptualised in the main as a survival strategy for individuals who, because their early relationships were

---

1   "Even when it's dark, I don't have to be lost." Lannowe Hall R & Parker Hall S, 2011, *Addiction Today, Even when it's dark, I don't have to be lost: Two therapeutic interventions for wilderness therapy at sea.* 5th International Adventure Therapy Conference 2012 BACP Research Conference 2012.

traumatic, did not experience 'good enough'[2] (Winnicott, 1965) early life support and as a consequence experienced developmental arrest. Most will not have successfully progressed through the first three developmental stages[3] (Clarke & Dawson, 1998) of Being, Doing and Thinking which roughly correlate to Erikson's (1950) stages (trust Vs mistrust and autonomy Vs shame and doubt); nor will they have received important affirmations that are crucial to Adult functioning.

SOK addressed the following developmental stages and conveyed the missing affirmations:

Stage	Task	Therapeutic Process	Examples of Affirmations required
First	Being	Encouraging awareness of sensual experience, physical sensations and emotional responses to the world	You can feel all of your feelings You can grow at your own pace
Second	Doing	The activity (sailing, cooking, cleaning)	You can explore and experiment and I will protect you You can use all your senses when you explore
Third	Thinking	Debriefing and processing experience to make meaning of it	You can think and feel at the same time You can know what you need and ask for help

---

2   'Good enough' (Winnicott, 1965). In 1960 Winnicott introduced on-site analysis, the idea of first true self and the false self. What Winnicott was careful to describe as good enough parenting, i.e. not necessarily perfect, the need for compliance with the parents' wishes and expectations. See clinical notes on disorders of childhood 1944.

3   Developmental stages (Clarke & Dawson, 1998) of Being, Doing and Thinking, which roughly correlate to Erikson's (1950) stages (trust Vs mistrust and autonomy Vs shame and doubt).

Overall, therapeutic interventions focus on developing an 'integrated adult'[4] (Berne, 1961), which incorporates the positive aspects of Parent and Child ego states. Clients connected with and strengthened their existing capacities for self-care (identifying needs, self-nurturing and setting limits), problem solving, developing competence and resilience and having fun. Through interventions like the two below, participants made use of the relationship between their body and their surroundings and engaged their physical, emotional and intuitive intelligence in order to better understand their current situation – an important skill for recovery.

Intervention one: Helming

The most basic activity of sailing a boat is taking the helm. In SOK, helming (steering the boat), to maintain a course and achieve one's objective, was carried out with the support of myself and possibly a peer. It required a participant to use their body as an instrument to gather information about their environment. They were invited to connect to themselves and their environment and to trust all the sensory information that is available including:

- what they could see
- what they could feel of the wind and/or sun on their face
- the feel of the motion of the boat (e.g. forward movement, resistance, heeling)
- the sound of the sails
- The feel of the helm and the tension of the helm against the rudder in direct contact with the sea.

Participants' Adult egos were strengthened as they incrementally increased their awareness of the relationship between their body, the boat and wider environment; and as they deepened trust in themselves to respond usefully as they progressed through the following stages:

---

4   'Integrated' (Berne, 1961) or 'integrating Adult' (Tudor, 2003)

Activity	Process	Developmental Task
Helming by sight	Relying on a fixed visual point; dependent on land and sight lines, spires, headlands etc. to achieve designated outcome	Mainly doing
Helming by compass	Relying on the compass and calculating the necessary adjustments to stay on course; the helm needs to be manoeuvred in the opposite direction to that anticipated.	Thinking and doing
Helming by sensing the wind (Zen)	Relying on how the wind impacts on face, body, sails and boat structure; course adjustments require intuitive body reflexes. This process involves a deeper connection with self and the environment and a process of 'letting go' of cognitive processes. The more a participant is at one with their environment, the more successful they are at maintaining their course. This is purely a process – the outcome is to maintain connection with the environment as that is the sole goal.	Doing and being

Activity	Process	Developmental Task
Blind helming	On day 3 or 4, after a period of orientation, a participant may be blindfolded and, supported by a peer, be asked to maintain a course (5-30 minutes). Trust in self and peer strengthened and usually the participant was amazed at how much their body assisted them in this process, at their ability to respond to the constantly changing conditions and to keep a course. It was all about staying in the process – staying connected, that is the goal.	Doing but mainly being

Participant comments:

Charlotte (blindfolded helmsman):

> "Incredible, I feel great... I never knew I could do that – I think I've achieved Jedi Knighthood."

Robert (blindfolded helmsman):

> "I think that now I can trust myself, all my senses, far more than I thought possible."

Trevor (blindfolded helmsman's buddy):

> "It was great to be trusted and listened to... I wasn't bossy either, I just gave the instructions."

There was often a great deal of reluctance to try blind helming, and yet remarkably enough, after some practice, many of the participants actually could maintain a straighter course than when they could see where they were going. I was often sitting next to them and giving simple instructions to keep it safe, mainly to maintain the wind at an appropriate angle. As I backed off and gave less verbal support, I found that the participant was no longer straining to look towards where they might be going, even though they were blindfolded. They would start to turn their head slightly towards the wind, sensing the changing direction of the wind as their guide. Sometimes they might be turned completely away from the course they were heading but completely in touch with the wind and the motion. I would often ask them if they had their eyes closed and, strangely enough, even though they had a blindfold on, they would usually reply in the affirmative.

Often, when starting to take the helm on the first day and follow a line of sight they would be tense and straining, trying too hard to get it right. They learned, step-by-step and exercise by exercise, to let go, stop trying, trust their bodies, and realise that their instincts (gut) would make good decisions. I would often say to them, "Here is a good time for you 'to get out of your head.'" Not in the way that they might have got out of their heads in their previous existence, but in a different way – to let their bodies do the talking. Possibly even to realise that their body cannot lie to them, and it is their mind that doesn't always tell them the truth, that it cannot always reflect reality as it is.

I remember an occasion when a participant really was making this connection during the blind helming exercise, becoming completely immersed in all the environmental changes going on around her. Sitting next to her I became acutely aware of how she felt energetically. This was not uncommon, as sometimes I would close my eyes and allow myself to sense, to feel energetically, how the helmsperson was, sensing this person sitting next to me. Occasionally, strong images came to mind, maybe an animal or a colour, but on this occasion, I had this sense of flying, of being on a broomstick – it was most extraordinary. I told her about this image and she responded by saying she also had had the sensation that she was on a broomstick, flying by the wind.

One of the difficulties occurring at an early stage of learning the different ways of helming and achieving one's goal can be when the helmsperson is asked to use the compass. It is counter-intuitive, as when helming by sight one turns the wheel in the direction you need the boat to go, but when helming by compass you do not turn the wheel in the direction the needle is pointing. This can be a difficult process for somebody who is dyslexic, where there appears to be a break between the left brain and the right brain coordination. I will elaborate on this in a later chapter when discussing neuroscience. This process of sailing by compass strengthens the coordination of left brain and right brain.

Intervention two: Night sailing

At night, *Physis* would motor sail from an anchorage out to sea and then SOK participants would navigate the boat back to another anchorage, a 2-to 3-hour journey. The passage was familiar in that they would have sailed there before in daylight, using obvious landmarks to navigate by such as headlands, spires, the lighthouse and large shipping anchored in the bay. These visual markers would not be visible at night; even the lighthouse appeared only as a flashing light amongst other flashing lights. The navigational light or a lighthouse light can vary in intensity and does not necessarily define the distance as it would do in daylight. They are now entering a world that is familiar but at the same time, completely different. To me, this is reminiscent of early recovery, where the world is experienced as fundamentally different and uncharted. It requires a new direction, different ways to chart progress and innovative tools to navigate through the ups and downs of living. My experience of early recovery was walking into and through Alice's looking glass: the world looked similar, but I didn't know how to navigate it. Old methods didn't work, and I had to find new ways to achieve my objectives.

Night sailing as a metaphor for the recovery process

Stages	Sailing	Recovery
1.	Consult a chart	Consult with those that have gone before you. A chart is like a manual; it is the self-help book written by people who'd been there before you. 12-Step programmes are a manual of how to proceed.
2.	Triangulate your position	Check in with yourself; what are you feeling and thinking? What do you need? Meditation, mindfulness.

Stages	Sailing	Recovery
3.	Plot your course to the destination including waypoints and points of reference	List your goals and plan your course of action; where necessary seek advice; identify how to measure your progress; 'one step at a time'
4.	Join the crew	You are not alone; friends, therapists, fellowships will all support you; you are an important support to others
5.	Check you have the necessary skills and equipment	Check you have the necessary tools and skills for your recovery, including emotional support, training, work, appropriate clothing, money, housing, relationships; use meditation, have some fun, get more information, ask for help and keep learning and growing
6.	Observe safety guidelines	Look after yourself; reduce risk
7.	List and tick off course changes	Mark your progress; share it with others again one step at a time, no shortcuts
8.	If in doubt, check your position	Reality-check, get feedback Stop, take a break, think it through
9.	If you lose your course, remember you are not back at the beginning of your journey; consult your chart, find your bearings, get back on course.	Relapse is part of the process: you are not back at the beginning; you have already come a long way; acknowledge your position, go back to stage one (but not square one) and re-commit to your recovery

Stages	Sailing	Recovery
10.	On reaching your destination ensure its suitable for anchoring; celebrate; rest a while before your next voyage	Ask yourself, "Is this where I want to be? Is this safe for me?" Congratulate yourself; take a break before you plan where to go next

Participants' comments:

Jonathan:

"Wow, that was exciting and scary and yet we got here safely"

Janice:

"That really works.... my recovery is just like that... everything is similar but different and I have to tackle things differently, and need help and different tools to do it"

Alan:

"I really liked that thing about one step at a time... if we had missed a step we would be on the rocks"

Pamela:

"Even when it's dark I don't have to be lost... all you have taught us was useful"

Both the interventions, helming and its variants, and night sailing, required participants' here-and-now Adult awareness. This can only emerge when a person is embodied (being), can reflect on their current state (thinking), and is able to take the appropriate action (doing), in order to respond to the ever-changing environmental conditions, make corrections to their course, resolve problems and achieve goals.

Experiential learning in process

For all this experience to have lasting benefits it needed to be integrated. All the exercises were debriefed and reflected on as they occurred, and further opportunity was provided to make meaning of the day's events in group 'process' time after the evening meal. Of course, mealtimes were also a great time to compare notes, reflect and enjoy one's successes.

Recovery is a personally demanding process. I argue that recovery and seafaring journeys require identical personal qualities and resources. I had a copy made of this statement to give to all my participants:

"When the conditions around you change, or your condition changes, you need to make some changes to maintain your course."

This is not only a truism about sailing but also a powerful metaphor for recovery, for life.

My Jedi Knight – Blind Helming

Adventures in the Woods

Sailing into the Light

'I don't think I have laughed so much'

'The therapy really moved me on I'm connected'

Heavy Sailing

Richard, 1980

Exercise in Levitation !!

Training at the Helm

Paperwork Evaluations

Richard, 2018

Male Group, 2016

10

Know the Ropes

Know the ropes: A sailor who 'knows the ropes' is familiar with the miles of cordage and ropes involved in running a ship.

Testimonials and feedback from residential agencies

It was important to obtain feedback from the residential agencies we were working with and quoted here are some of the highlights of the evaluation reports over the first few years. These evaluations were helpful in assessing the value of our work, and, due to their positive nature, they were used in funding applications.

Brief quotes taken from residential and care managers' reports

The residential care managers were asked to complete evaluation reports at the end of each year. Here are some excerpts from these reports, received between 2011 and 2016.

Participants:

- develop and increase resilience and a sense of wellbeing
- develop negotiation skills and an increase in self-awareness
- develop a positive and practical experience of interdependency

- come to understand the need for teamwork and co-operation with each another
- always return with a sense of achievement
- get a feeling of hope
- experience being part of a team and learn to resolve issues, and manage conflict
- have transformative experiences which enhances their development of the spiritual aspects of their recovery
- are allowed to simply "be"
- describe having transpersonal experiences
- learn new skills
- get a very concrete experience to draw on and from which to recognise resilience, existing strengths and the ability to make positive changes in their lives
- report having had a positive experience of themselves, increased confidence, self-awareness, improved communication skills, and a lot of gratitude, and having had a lot of fun
- have a greatly increased sense of their own potential to have a productive and useful life when they leave residential treatment
- who have this unique experience dramatically increase their chances of remaining drug/alcohol free. To conclude, each session's limited numbers encourage openness, and enhance the above changes due to being in smaller, more intimate and sometimes challenging groups. This is a unique and excellent therapeutic intervention given the short and intense time-period of the sessions and the achievements and outcomes reported are remarkable.

Feedback from 2012 manager therapist at Ocean Quays, Wendy Van-de-Niet

"The Sailaday OK session/s play an important role in the healing process and integrates well into our treatment plan. Historical abuse and trauma triggers feelings of intense helplessness, fear, and lack of control – an opportunity to engage in a practical activity, in a safe and supportive environment, challenges these feelings. It gives a very concrete experience to draw on and from which to recognise resilience, existing strengths and the ability to make positive changes in their lives.

This is a very important part of someone's treatment now and of their personal development and having this opportunity and this unique experience dramatically increases their chances of remaining drug/alcohol free and to work with their underlying issues. Those that have had the Sailaday experience have been more likely to complete treatment."

It was great to receive all this positive and constructive feedback. In turn, I saw it as my responsibility to flag up any relevant issues back to counselling teams. The intensity of these four days left the participants vulnerable and it always seemed important to me that they had a safe and supportive environment to return to. I would give a written report to the counselling team which was fairly minimal as everything that happened on the boat was confidential. This report was written in collaboration with the resident. If there was some important issue that their counsellor needed to know about I would have discussed this first with the resident.

Feedback and testimonials from agencies 2011/13

Question: The main aim of Sailaday OK is for the participants "to have a positive experience of themselves": please give feedback.

"Most clients have come back having had a positive experience; they have also faced their fears and overcome them. They have discovered new things about themselves and increased their confidence. They have got to know each other better". Broadreach 2011

Question: How has Sailaday OK been helpful for your clients?

"Increased confidence, self-awareness, learning to sail and associated aspects, communication skills, relationship building, manage conflict, facing fears, trying something new, new passions, gratitude, self-discovery, team building, learning to sail, community and communication, building trust, positive experience, natural buzz/high of the whole experience". (2012)

Question: Are there any specific positive changes that you have been aware of for the participants?

"How to manage conflict, relationship building, team building, and new experience, more confident and more willing to enter into the processes."

Derek Buchanan – Longreach residential manager 2014:

"The primary benefits for our clients arise from the opportunity to understand the need for teamwork and for working in close co-operation with one another. Clients have often only known dependent or co-dependent relationships in the past and their experience of four days together at sea provides a positive and practical experience of interdependency. Their interpersonal skills are tested as they need to overcome any difficulties that arise between them whilst at sea.

They always return with a sense of achievement – they are often apprehensive beforehand about how they will cope with such a new experience and to have successfully overcome their fears and completed the task leaves them feeling confident and ready to take on the world. They get a feeling of hope. Being on board the boat for four days allows clients to leave their problems behind and allows them to simply "be", whilst focused on the business of sailing and not worrying about responsibilities in their daily lives outside of treatment. Clients frequently describe having transpersonal experiences especially when at the helm and during night sailing. This is often transformative and allows many clients to continue to address spiritual aspects of their recovery. They have a greatly increased sense of their own potential to have a productive and useful life when they leave residential treatment".

Charles Howard-Baker – Closereach residential manager 2014:

"The primary benefits are team building, learning to resolve issues, learning to manage conflict, looking at things in a new way, building relationships with each other, building trust and confidence and self-esteem. They learn to sail and learn new skills of meditation and mindfulness in a beautiful environment. Being able to sit with self can be challenging and learning to manage new challenges increases their resilience.

What is unique to the SOK experience is they manage to achieve the above due to being in smaller, more intimate and sometimes challenging groups. The smaller numbers encourage openness. The relaxing, exhilarating, dramatic environment of the sea, to spend time away from Closereach supports them in their search to find themselves and gives them a new and different perspective on their life. This is an experiential way of learning and seems to make a significant positive difference. This new perspective opens new opportunities and new interests and a feeling of hope, which is fundamental to their development."

Amanda McCann[1] Addaction 2015. Here, Amanda is reporting on a session for young people who were negatively affected by their carer's addiction:

"We see Sailaday as an excellent therapeutic intervention to support our families in their journeys to make significant changes to their lives and to the lives of their families.

This is a unique programme. Many of our families would otherwise not have an opportunity to explore strengths and weaknesses of family dynamics, to develop and increase resilience through activity and apparent risk taking, and to work on negotiation skills and an increase in self-awareness.

It also gives families an opportunity to explore and improve communication skills and to have fun together, whilst increasing self-esteem, trust and openness. Finally, to experience co-operation and a more positive attitude toward each other. This is where we see the strengths of this experience and the positive effects that this can have on each and every member of the families involved."

Andrew Ferguson 2016: Schools Substance Awareness project worker YZUP (Young Person's Substance Misuse Team):

"Good morning Richard

Firstly, a big thank you for yesterday, I thought it was a fantastic experience and after talking to the young people they got a lot from it. Some were able to vocalise this more than others, but all gave positive feedback in their own way. I personally found it amazing and I don't mind saying it came at a good time for me, practising the mindfulness and just sitting on the front of the boat really helped me focus on the now... so I thank you for that. I had the lyrics of a song in my head all yesterday evening, 'The ocean looks like a thousand diamonds strewn across a blue blanket, I lean against the wind,

---

1   Addaction: is a British charity founded in 1967 which supports people to make positive behavioural changes mostly from alcohol and drug abuse. They work with all ages and the carers.

pretend that I am weightless and in this moment I am happy'... Thought it was very appropriate (Wish you were here by Incubus)

Regarding the day I will firstly say that your calm manner worked very well with the young people, from the outset allowing them to use any area of the boat, to walk freely was a good thing and not be confined to one area, this gave an instant feeling of trust. The fact that nothing was compulsory was also a winner. The mindfulness was great and although it was disrupted this was appreciated by the two females of the group. I would suggest that following the initial introduction to mindfulness that there are other options throughout the day to do this again, whether this be as a group or just hints that they could go off by themselves to other parts of the boat and practice it.

The actual controlling of the boat and putting sails up and down was definitely the highlight for the YPs. It's not often you get to 'control' something of that size in an 'uncontrollable' environment – loved all the comparisons to life – again, this worked well with the ladies, however 'H' is a very matter of fact young man and metaphor and analogies don't work too well with him, although that being said he got a great deal without fully realising it – I work with 'H' and he has a very 'instant gratification' outlook on things – this was a good exercise in delaying gratification for him.

Regarding the length of the day, I feel it was pitched right – I was thinking about this in some detail and thinking about tailoring it slightly to fit 'internalised' and 'externalised' characteristics – maybe reducing the length of time for those who struggle with attention and concentration, but actually I feel the length of time and amount of activities is right for both. The balance of doing things and actually just sitting with 'yourself' is spot on.

Loved the fact we got to swim – this should be made an optional feature of the day. Lunch was lovely and the consultation forms in advance asking for specific requests from the young people were again a winner.

The blog at the end would've been great – maybe set up a camera in a 'diary room' style (hate the fact I'm thinking of the show Big Brother, as I'm not a fan)... if the camera was set up throughout the day, the YPs could go down there as and when they feel – this would allow less focus on them as I think they felt embarrassed to do it in front of each over and also by the end of the day they aren't as motivated... Also, a list of possible things they could talk about – just *hints, i.e. best bits, worst bits, most challenging, any funny moments etc, but also still maintaining they can talk about whatever they like.*

I hope some of this helps... anything else, give me a shout, I'd be happy to help..."

2012 Manager – Plymouth Residential:

"This is a very important part of someone's treatment now and in their personal development and having this opportunity and this unique experience dramatically increases their chances of remaining drug/alcohol free and to work with their underlying issues."

2013 Manager therapist, Ocean Quay Plymouth:

'The Sailaday OK session/s play an important role in the healing process and integrate well into our treatment plan. Historical abuse and trauma triggers feelings of intense helplessness, fear, and lack of control – an opportunity to engage in a practical activity, in a safe and supportive environment, challenges these feelings. It gives a very concrete experience to draw on and from which to recognise resilience, existing strengths and the ability to make positive changes in their lives".

Here seems a good place to include some of the factualized narratives from participants. These derive from written evaluations, formal and informal interviews after the event.

Female, aged 31, 2011

Early triggers were abuse; a violent alcoholic father; parental domestic violent abuse; *"...abuse throughout my whole life"*. Consequences were feeling unloved, unimportant, useless. *"...useful only for CCF, as my ex-boyfriend used to call it – cooking, cleaning and f***ing."*

"My life before treatment: Difficult, despairing, home detox; methadone, lived alone; had to do it quickly due to lack of time. Family and friends issues; felt

I was worthless, was there only for pleasure or use of others. (Lower than a snake's belly).

What effects Sailaday had? The first trip, I dealt with an extremely difficult situation and that was the start of me talking to others about the abuse and getting real. The second trip allowed me or kind of forced me to recognise the progress I'd made in treatment. Acknowledging my progress/success has always been hard.

Life now: OK. Some tough days but keep busy at Ocean Quay (day centre) 5 days a week; learned much since leaving Longreach about myself. I am still learning, still have much to learn, but I feel OK. I've recently had four days in a row where I felt content, never felt content before – it feels good!! It's possible!!! That is great. I still do EMDR, so that can be tough, especially in the evenings, living alone, but I have all the support round me I need, some great people who care, who accept me as I am and that is teaching me slowly to accept me as I am too. I'm learning it's OK to make mistakes, it won't kill me and it doesn't make me a bad person (still learning that), but it's OK, OK is good, it's better than shit-faced and "lower than a snakes belly". Sailaday open the door for me – I really don't think I'd be here today without that experience, thank you."

The following account is from an addict/alcoholic. Privileged education and upbringing; and, as he would say: *"...addiction is no respecter of class or social standing."* 56, male chronic, multiple addictions.

"I never knew a time when I didn't want to be somebody else, when I felt I didn't belong, and a distorted sense of self, and certainly always felt there was something wrong with me. I felt then a deep sense of shame of being me. God help me, everyone could see below the façade, my facade was good, I thought!!

I was a functioning addict until the last years, an addict/alcoholic and then I lost my health, family, marriage, home and business. I have drunk for as long as I was able, finishing the leftovers at parents' parties as young as 10. At 17 I wanted the life of 'drugs, sex, and rock n' roll' (1967) and I found it. 25 years of heroin addiction followed and large quantities of alcohol and any other drug I could get my hands on.

This took me down a path of anti-social behaviour and criminal activity to pay for my addiction and for the adrenaline rush. I stole from my family, children, business and friends. By the end I was physically, emotionally and spiritually crippled and incapable of functioning.

Finally, I realized I might die, I had had many near-death experiences and thanks to the health service returned to the living, but until the end I believed I would get away with it. I then made a decision to live. I wanted life.

Today I am fully functioning, aware, responsible and an honest individual. I know love and am able to love. I feel fulfilled and gratitude for the life I have. I have moments of peace and happiness.

My recovery would not be what it is today if I hadn't had the experiences of sailing and that connection with the elements. I learnt through sailing to trust my body – it does not lie to me, plus an ability to assess problems and feel the self-esteem in solving them. The most difficult place for me had been to accept the present for exactly what it is and listen and trust it (it had always seemed safer to be in the past or future). This is a prerequisite for successful sailing in order to achieve goals. To do this I need to know where I am where I am going and how I am going to get there. If the conditions, or my condition, changes I need to make changes and, if necessary, let go of the goal and move in sympathy with the world around me.

Being at sea has opened a door for me, this sense of a connection to the world around me and to myself and has become the basis for a more spiritual way of living."

I love the quotation below, from Arturo Perez-Reverte, Spanish journalist and writer, written in 1951. It shows how another person experiences being at sea.

"The land lies behind him, and everything he could need was travelling with him, circumscribed by the tight limits of the ship. At sea, he thought, men travelled with their houses on their backs, like the knapsack of the explorer or the shell that moves with the snail. All you need is a few gallons of diesel, sails, and a favourable wind, for everything that dry land provided to become superfluous, dispensable. Voices, noises, smells, the tyranny of the clock had no meaning here. To sail out until the coast falls behind your stern – that was

one goal met. Facing the menacing and magical presence of the omnipresent sea, sorrow, desire, sentimental attachments, hatreds and hopes dissolve in the wake, dwindling until they seem far away, meaningless, because the ocean brings people back to themselves. There are things which are unbearable on shore – thoughts, absences, anguishes – can only be borne on the deck of the ship. There is no painkiller as strong as that. Men survive on ships who would have lost their reason and tranquillity forever anywhere else. Course, wind, waves, position, and the days run, survival; out there these are the only words that have meaning. Because it is true that the real freedom, the only possible freedom, the true peace of God, begins five miles from the nearest coast."

Arturo Perez-Reverte, 1951, Spanish journalist and writer

11

The Sea is the Perfect
Metaphor for Life

'The sea is the perfect metaphor for life.' [1] *Martin*

I WAS INVITED to Czechoslovakia for the Seventh International Conference of Adventure Therapists. My presentation, which I co-wrote with Ms. Sue Parker Hall MSc, UKCP, was entitled: 'Sailing as a metaphor for life; exploring the transformational experiences of a marine adventure therapy and how these transfer to life ashore.'

Nautical phrases in common usage:

- *'Nail one's colours to the mast'*
- *'Plain sailing'*
- *'All hands to the pumps'*
- *'Take a different tack'*
- *'Plumbing the depths'*
- *'I'm alright Jack'*
- *'Sailing too close to the wind'*
- *'Falling in the drink'*
- *'Sorry to cut across your bows'*
- *'All hands on deck'*

- *'Being cut adrift'*
- *'Stop rocking the boat'*
- *'Took the wind out of my sails'*
- *'Flying the flag'*
- *'In the doldrums'*
- *'Weathering a storm'*
- *'Being all at sea'*
- *'Waiting to see which way the wind is blowing'*
- *'Paddling my own canoe'*

---

1 ???

- 'Welcome aboard, coming aboard, all aboard'
- 'Time and tide awaits for no man'
- 'Leave some leeway'

- 'Throw caution to the winds'
- 'Keep one hand for the ship and one hand for yourself'
- 'Take on board'

An excerpt from the abstract of my presentation is as follows:

"This presentation will use video clips combined with concepts from Transactional Analysis to show how Sailaday OK's four days and nights marine adventure therapy programme aboard a yacht integrates the healing potential of the natural environment with psychotherapy to provide a transformational experience that supports the recovery of those who have experienced addiction, abuse and other traumas."

It was another great experience going to this conference – Paradise Park is about a hundred square miles of protected landscape, mountains, forests and lakes situated not far south of the Polish border. It was another chance to integrate with other therapists from all over the world and to renew some friendships with people I had met in Edinburgh.

It was interesting to find that there was at least one other presentation referring to the use of metaphors and how important it is to use one's thinking to make sense of the experience, recognising that this is how you integrate the experience. I also found that a large majority of people, particularly those who were having to chase funding, were also struggling with how to collect and to present qualitative as well as quantitative evaluations and feedback. We all understood that it was not an adequate evaluation to simply say that this person got a job, or that this person stayed out of prison for such and such an amount of time. We were offering so much more, so how could we get this message across? I was a little envious to find that many of our American peers were receiving good state funding.

We needed quantitative and qualitative research data evidence demonstrating how participants had experienced and benefited from the Sailaday OK experience and how they had then integrated their learning into life ashore. We were at that time trying to set up some sort of programme for collecting evaluations for the period 1 to 5 years after their session with SOK. This was difficult, as many of our clients were still pretty chaotic, often changing address and moving about the country. We were partially successful in undertaking some telephone interviews, but our main source of feedback was our RATs (Returnee Adventure Therapees) mentoring groups. I was looking forward to an exchange of ideas with colleagues at the conference about how to assess the sustainability of these changes over the longer term.

My presentation went something like this:

Sailing is understood as a metaphor for life. The process of acclimatising to ever-changing landscapes, sea states and weather conditions is likened to the need to adjust to the ongoing emotional and practical challenges of life. Quantitative and qualitative research data will be presented that evidence how participants experience and benefit from the Sailaday OK experience and how they integrate their learning into life ashore.

Our participants are recovering from chemical addictions, abuse and trauma and are in the potentially difficult transition from intensive residential drug and alcohol treatment centres to living in the community. We sail from Falmouth, Cornwall, UK for 4/5 days and nights at a time, and in groups of 4.

From my own experience, "I understand addiction as a coping mechanism for trauma, usually archaic, dating back to early life" (RH). We understand that "trauma arrests the development of, or undermines the functioning of, an individual's Adult ego state" (Berne, 1957). When traumatised, we can only respond to today's events in a way that is unhelpfully influenced by our past.

Addiction serves to keep raw, unprocessed emotional experience out of awareness because of an inability to process it, to feel it through, to come to terms with what has happened. Unfortunately, people who are traumatised are not only unable to process the experience which afflicted them in the first place but frequently have been unable to process many subsequent life events, resulting in a multiple pile-up of emotional experience which has never been expressed.

I came to understand from neuroscience that, "in order to process trauma, both left and right brain need to be engaged at the same time" (Schore, 1994). EMDR[2] (Shapiro, 1989, 2012) uses bilateral stimulation (eye movement or taps) because you cannot *not* process whatever material you are focusing on when both right brain and left brain are being stimulated at the same time.

Bi-lateral stimulation can happen in other ways; for example, through experiencing an empathic relationship which encourages the processing of emotion through using left brain language to express right brain experience; this is at the heart of psychotherapy. It also occurs when sailing; steering

---

2   EMDR (Shapiro, 1989, 2012) Shapiro F, 1989, Efficacy of the eye movement desensitisation procedure in the treatment of traumatic memories, Journal of Traumatic Stress, 2, 199-223

and using a compass often involves behaving counter-intuitively and in performing any task aboard you need to think and feel at the same time.

It seems absolutely clear to me that when combining an empathic psychotherapeutic relationship with sailing, this creates the best possible environment for stimulating change.

"The ocean brings people back to themselves."[3] Del Guado

This capacity is a primary function of the integrating Adult ego state[4] (Tudor, 2002) and, once developed, a person can then deal with the backlog of unprocessed archaic emotional material that was lodged in their Child ego state. As a result, their Adult ego state is strengthened and expanded; the energy which was used to repress the organism's trauma is now available to them in the here-and-now. They are more present to their experience, more able to reflect on their present situation and to think usefully and feel at the same time. They are better able to do the necessary emotional processing in any given situation, to weigh up their circumstances accurately, to realistically assess risk and make good decisions about what is required to proceed safely and effectively. This capacity greatly improves people's view of themselves and so it increases their confidence and self-esteem. They are more likely to feel, *"I'm OK, you're OK"*,[5] and to be able to negotiate, collaborate and work as a team.

At the end of a session, participants often expressed relief and a renewed vigour, energy, hopefulness, willingness and preparedness to now step out, deal with the stuff that was still hanging about and move on. Often I would hear them say: *"I want to live, I feel I've got a life now"*.

Gibran[6] (1923) uses powerfully and persuasively the metaphor of sailing to articulate the 'integrating Adult ego state' (Tudor, 2002) in action, with the right brain and left brain operating in unison. He speaks to us of reason and passion:

"Your reason and passion are the rudder and the sails of your seafaring soul.

If either your sails or your rudder be broken, you can but toss and drift, or else be held at a standstill in mid-seas.

---

3 Del Guado, Spanish writer and mariner 1923
4 Integrating Adult ego state; Berne, 1961 or 'integrating' (Tudor, 2002)
5 "I'm OK, you're OK", Berne 1961
6 Gibran K, 1923, *The Prophet*, Alfred A Knopf, New York

Reason, ruling alone, is a force confining; and passion, unattended, is a flame that burns to its own destruction."

I find the metaphor a useful way of condensing and communicating complex ideas. In psychotherapy it is used to engage the Adult ego state in a reflecting process and to think and make meaning of experiences (right brain and left brain functioning together).

I certainly understand the power of sailing as a metaphor that is steeped in useful wisdom that is easily transferrable to recovery from addiction and to life in general. Staying afloat and managing ever-changing weather, sea and emotional states, often beyond an individual's control, requires the same high degree of Adult present awareness, ability to reflect and make meaning and to manage emotional experience, as does adjusting to the ongoing practical and emotional challenges of recovery and life.

When working at the helm I would often remind people: "When the conditions around you change you need to make adjustments and changes". As when the wind or seas alter you need to make the appropriate adjustments, so when your condition changes you need to make adjustments. In sailing terms – if you get cold you need to pull on a jersey, if you need a pee, again you need to make suitable arrangements. So, "When the conditions around you change you need to make changes, and when your condition changes you need to adapt". This is a fairly simple metaphor for life and not just sailing.

All the exercises and interventions are designed to expand and strengthen the integrating Adult, which we understand to be arrested when a person is traumatised and/or using alcohol and drugs.

My job as skipper-facilitator is to model an integrating Adult by being authentic, boundaried and to maintain safety. In Rogerian terms I strive to create the optimum environment in which an organism can grow and thrive[7] (Rogers, 1980); I attempt to engender the conditions in which both left-brain and right-brain activity are bilaterally stimulated. I need to contextualise and direct the exercise and encourage participants to notice and reflect on their thoughts and feelings. These are both the more debilitating archaic feelings that are not congruent to the immediate task such as powerlessness, uselessness and stupidity as well as appropriate feelings in the moment, for example, a degree of anxiety, fear and excitement. Also ensuring continuing encouragement to take pleasure in the 'wow!' factor, the thrill of the experience, an enjoyment in the pleasure of achieving and connecting.

---

7   Carl Rogers creator of person-centred psychotherapy, Roger area psychotherapy. Person centred therapy seeks to facilitate clients self-actualising tendency i.e. see *Physis*; Carl Rogers 1942 *Counselling and Psychotherapy* ISBN 978-1406760873

This tick list is as relevant for a sailing journey as it is for an existential or actual journey:

- Have I considered where I am (my starting point) and identified my goal?
- Is this goal achievable?
- A chart is like a manual, a narrative, written by those who have made the journey before; a therapist, mentor or sponsor can help us to complete a successful voyage.
- A course is prepared one step (waypoint) at a time. 12-Step Fellowship Programmes will encourage you to manage your new life and recovery one day at a time.
- Have I considered my condition? Am I fit, physically, emotionally and mentally? Do I have the means, the resources and the tools?
- Am I prepared to ask for help and to co-operate?
- Do I have the flexibility required? Do I accept that when the conditions change, I need to make some changes or that if my condition changes, I need to respond?
- How will I know when I have achieved my goal?

SOK collected quantitative and qualitative data to measure effectiveness and to develop the project. The quantitative data was generated by feedback forms.

SOK is a process and a phenomenological experience, so we also want to understand the unique meaning that each individual takes from it. As a result, we also collect qualitative data through asking some open questions which invite their reflection.

To help us to make meaning of the quantitative and qualitative data, SOK collaborated with a number of expert bodies: the universities of Plymouth and Exeter's European Centre for Environment and Human Health; a research fellow from University of Plymouth, and with the National Marine Aquarium. We were keen to identify the benefits to well-being to be gained from the 'Blue Gym' studies.

The following are samples of themes from 2011 (*Qualitative Evaluation 2010/11 Report* Dr Katherine Ashbullby) extracted from her thorough qualitative and quantitative analysis of our evaluations.

There are some common themes which emerged from the feedback obtained by SOK from its clients:

The feeling of belonging (Extract 40/60); *Found peace within myself* (Extract 35/60); *The whole experience! It was unique, inspiring + honest good fun* (Extract 55/60); *The therapy helped me move forward* (Extract 33/60); *The night-time sailing was brilliant – it was the same journey as in daytime but felt totally different at night. It was calm and peaceful* (Extract 53/60); *The teamwork and bonding were good* (Extract 37/60); *The fact that we all worked as team* (Extract 41/60); *Really helpful understanding sailing as a metaphor for my recovery* (Extract 39/60).

Finally, Jeremy Holmes'[8] (1993) sailing metaphor describes both the process and outcomes of psychotherapy but can equally be applied to sailing and recovery from addiction:

"On weighing the anchor, every sailor must take with him the best possible technical and cultural equipment for coping with the perils of the sea, but the expert sailor knows that he must adapt his techniques to the sea and the weather and that every voyage will to some extent be unpredictable and at any rate different from its predecessors. It is precisely this awareness, no less than the skills acquired that distinguishes his approach from the rigid illusions nurtured by the beginner."

---

8   Jeremy Holmes, British psychotherapist, see John Bowlby and *Attachment Theory* 1993 Routledge, ISBN 9780415077293

12

Taken Aback

Taken aback: On a square-rigger the sails were 'taken aback' when the wind was blowing on the wrong side of the sails, causing a dangerous situation, or backing the sails to ride out a storm.

SAILING IS GENERALLY about using what is available in terms of wind and sea to get from one place to the other. The idea is to use the sails to propel you along; you adjust the alignment of the sails with respect to the apparent wind direction and mobilise this power to steer a course.

My first lesson to participants was on how to use the motor to steer a course; they would steer towards a given point using the line of sight. This was followed by an exercise in how to maintain a course by using a magnetic compass. Then there would be similar exercises using the sails. All these exercises were about achieving a specific outcome, getting to a particular place or position on a chart. At some point in the following days, I would contract with them to take part in a slightly different exercise – Zen sailing.

Zen sailing is purely sailing to wind; to keep the wind at a particular angle to the boat, so that the sails will be set accordingly to achieve the best possible motion, speed and manoeuvrability. There is no set point of arrival; it is all about the journey and the process.

The helmsman, and the crew in support (adjusting sail tension etc), needed to tune in to the conditions around them and keep them constant. To keep the wind at that specific angle, to maintain the pressure of the rudder against the sea, to feel the motion of the boat, to feel the wind on skin, to tune in and let your body be the instrument. I was not asking them to maintain a perfect course or arrive at some specific place on the horizon – I was asking them to stop thinking and let their bodies do the sailing.

On occasion, this was a prelude to undertaking blind helming, when the helmsperson is blindfolded.

My experience of early recovery was realising that one part of my body was quite disconnected from the other. At times I felt I was fragmenting and being swept along uncontrollably. I came to accept that this was mostly in my mind; my body and my body/mind/sense were perfectly capable of holding me steady if only I could trust them. I learned from sailing that when I turned off some of the clutter and chatter in my head and let my body do the sailing, I was far more effective.

I wanted these participants to have the learning experience which made them aware that their bodies were instruments worth listening to. Their senses and feelings were there to help them, not to make life more difficult. The question that often came up during group processing was: *"What is the point of having all these feelings and why in early treatment do we have 'feelings' groups?"* To answer this, I asked them to return in their mind's eye to their Zen sailing experience and notice that everything they were sensing was helpful information. Unlike during active addiction when feelings are tempered by the chemical and the effect is that helpful information is drowned out and overwhelmed. Today you are waking up and it's not always comfortable.

The feelings I remember most from early recovery are the physical pain and emotional distress. I could not differentiate one from the other. I knew I was starting to recover when I could put names to different feelings or different sensations; I could tell the difference between grief and anger. Some of it was archaic – for example, what someone had said or done to me to make me angry in the past, and some was in the here and now. I needed to know the difference between that and the rage I felt from past experiences. I had to learn to separate this, as part of my growth of resilience, and if I could stay with the difficult feelings long enough, they began to make sense and my resilience developed. These sailing exercises were resilience training.

I would wake up in the mornings and very quickly notice all the little aches and pains, the discomforts, tricky and difficult thoughts and feelings; I probably had quite a long list. Occasionally I would wake up feeling okay, even maybe quite good, but I didn't have many words to describe okayness, happiness or joy. I suggest that, like you and other addicts in recovery, I had a vast capacity for emotional and physical sensations and pain. However, I believe, due to these and other similar exercises, I started to differentiate and make sense of what I was feeling. I could then explore these feelings one at a time instead of experiencing an overwhelming mass trying to blow me away. Eventually, the positive feelings expanded and developed.

The feedback from these exercises was often similar. Female participants, in particular, profited quickly from them because I found that they were more likely to retain a negative physical self-image which would have been derived by a history of abuse, trauma and cultural indoctrination.

Examples of feedback:

"Certainly, didn't think I could do this, but I learnt that my body is a friend and a powerful ally."

"I've always hated my body – it's been my enemy, shamed of my body, but today I feel different, something has changed, and I like it."

The experiential exercises used in our programme of marine adventure therapy had consisted of blind-helming, Zen sailing, night sailing, and different methods of helming (steering the boat) to develop left brain/right brain coordination, all helping to expand connection with the sense of Self and the environment. In 2017 I increased this programme to include one new exercise, based on one I had used in sailing training. Participants were taught to stop the boat at any given point, using sailing skills not motorised skills. The process involved using personal skills on the helm, the crew, the sails, and a developing personal awareness of all the environmental issues of wind, sea and tide. You use what you are given by making a direct connection with the environment, using nature to bring the boat into a state of stillness. Ideally, we would practise this process, firstly in calm waters and then in increasingly disturbed environments.

On a practical level, you may wish to bring the boat to a halt to pick up a mooring, a casualty or as a useful way of riding out a storm. The sailing term is 'hove-to', bringing the boat to 'irons' by fault or on purpose. By lashing the helm in opposition to the sails, the boat will gradually come to rest, ride the storm, head into the oncoming sea, or gently drift, depending on conditions.

This is a mindful process; being mindful of your physicality, your nature and your spirit, and to use your thinking to bring all these elements into alignment in order to find stillness. This experiential way of learning can be seen as a metaphor, and a transferable skill.

Of course, the boat, like one's self, can never be utterly stationary. One is in a perpetual state of motion and, as with Tai Chi, which is the art of being perfectly balanced while in a state of perpetual motion, the practising of this has many benefits to mind, body and spirit – and some might say to one's very soul. This connection to nature was the essence of the Sailaday

Experience, bringing about an experiential connection with one's own nature. Nature doesn't just exist outside of ourselves; we *are* nature, and the benefits of immersion in nature, emotionally, mentally, physically and spiritually are well-documented.

Neuroplasticity refers to changes and growth in neural pathways and synapses due to changes in behaviour, environment, neural processes, thinking, and emotions. Neuroplasticity has replaced the formerly held position that the brain is a physiologically static organ. Present research shows that the brain changes throughout life, that it is in a state of perpetual change. A positive relationship with another person increases the process of growth, of neoplasticity. I have experienced, and come to understand, that this also happens when we have a positive empathic experience with nature.

Immersion in the environment can bring you to a state of stillness, calm and peace. This challenge of bringing the boat to a state of stillness required the exercising of practical skills and taking on experiential learning of the process. It is not an easy exercise to get right, to become good at; it takes practice, and I didn't expect my participants to get anywhere near achieving that, but after some trials they managed to experience the possibilities.

A common reaction from participants introduced to this exercise was, *"All right Richard, but where are the brakes?"* Quite rightly so, but my answer was that they would be learning to use what they were given, what they had at their disposal to bring about some stability.

They would have been taught tricks in their early recovery to help them to keep their feet on the ground. It would have been suggested that they take one day at a time, focus on serenity, communicate with others and tell them what they were thinking and feeling. Mine was an exercise for them to experience stillness and peace even when it feels impossible, even when there is noise, unsteady motion and feelings of apparent risk all about you, and yet you can use all these elements to help bring you to stillness.

Quotes and feedback:

"I'm left with a new sureness in my options and balance. I chuckle as I notice how spending time standing on the boat on the water has left me better connected with the solid ground under my feet. I feel now more able to deal with the roar and stress of life – I have a choice."

"The day has left me with a deeper trust in my ability to choose my direction, to take a bearing, and relax in the movement towards it, an ability to step back and take 'a knee'."

"The experience of finding stillness when all around appears chaotic noise and stress gives me the ability to no longer have to flee or fight: I have a great new tool."

"It's a potent combination – being gently and quietly invited to pay attention to body experience, to emotion, thought and other experience, to relax and to trust, and to combine this with being in active physical relationship with the very real pull of wind, water, wood and sail, noise and movement."

This part of Cornwall offers a wide range of environments to sail in, with protected estuaries or wider stretches of ocean further away from land, depending on conditions and the quality of experience of your crew. I love the creeks that are so beautiful, quiet and safe for anchorage and to spend the night. Helford estuary is one of those beauty spots, with secret creeks hidden by ancient oak woods. It is a favourite of mine for night anchorage and I can't think of a better place to wake up and practise our early morning meditation than the area of Frenchman's Creek.

Once, we were hiding further up the estuary, as there was quite a storm brewing out to sea, and I recognised over on the south bank a quay known as Tremayne Quay. An ancient stopping off place once upon a time, when there were trading vessels going up and down the estuary, it is in a remote piece of country surrounded by steep banked woodland, lazy paths and at times noisy wildlife. When the wind blew through the trees it was quite an orchestra of sounds. There were no shops, off-licences, McDonald's or pubs anywhere near, so I thought it might be a good place to tie up and offer my group a walk in the woods.

There was a purpose to this exercise, and there were rules for everyone to adhere to. They were expected to return to the boat within an hour. They were encouraged to notice all the differences, smells, sounds and the feeling of walking on land, and they were asked to find and bring back an object. A 'found object' from the woods – only one of them, it had to fit in a pocket, and it needed to be dead. In other words, no tree branches, rabbits, or the like. I suggested that on their walk they would find and be drawn to some object and just to notice the circumstances in which that happened, bring it back and we would talk about it later as a group. I had experienced this once before with a group in Czechoslovakia, facilitated by an experienced mountain guide who was an adventure therapist, and I had been impressed with it; I just hoped I had remembered it right.

So off they went, on this blustery windy, showery day, mostly quite willingly except for a few grumbles from Fred. Fred thought I was just trying to get rid of them all for an hour so I could have a bit of peace and quiet. He was partly right, but it also gave me an opportunity to clean the toilet and cooker – the skipper's work is never done!

To my relief, within an hour, they returned to the boat singly or in pairs, showing off their 'found objects'. I asked them to lay them carefully on the table in the main cabin, as they would be the centrepiece for our group that evening. Fred said he would start, and with a flourish, a giggle and a cheeky grin, he showed his object to everybody. He held up his 'bottle top' and, with a hint of aggression, he turned to me and, to my recollection, the conversation went as follows:

"What you gonna make of that then, eh?"

"Okay Fred, so where was it and how did you come across it?"

"Well, it was just lying there in the path and just looked a bit out of place. I wasn't going to get some silly flower or feather or something like I think you wanted me to."

"That's cool Fred, can you describe it please so everybody can hear what you can see."

"Okay, I think it's a beer bottle top, it's a bit dirty on the inside, a bit muddy, and the edges are serrated and a bit sharp, the outside looks old and must have be shiny once, it's just an old bottle top, make something of that then..." he sniggered.

"It's not really the sort of thing you'd find in the woods, it is as you say a bit out of place, can you pass it to me please let me have a look, and can I tell you what I can see."

He passed it to me, and the rest of the group were intrigued and quieter. They had been giggling with Fred but by now they had sort of calmed down and were showing more interest. I held the object carefully in my hands, turned it around several times and inspected it with care. I treated it with respect and there was a hush in the cabin.

"I'm not surprised you found this object Fred, and that it attracted you, and I have to say that I rather suspect at first glance you were thinking of taking the piss a little bit, having a bit of a giggle having a bit of a laugh at Richard's expense." There was a nod and grin from Fred. "But I guess it stood out as a little bit different, a little unexpected, didn't quite fit with all the earthy colours and textures. And yet there it was – part of the landscape, a little downtrodden, a little bit bent and little bit discoloured, a little bit of a has-been."

Fred's expression was changing. A shadow, possibly of anger, flitted across his face, and then he relaxed and looked thoughtful. I continued to look at it and hold it up for everyone to see.

"I find it interesting that the inside and the outside are so different, the outside is slightly tarnished, but it was clearly once a beautiful colour and shiny. In fact, if I wipe it, the shine comes back, look! Not quite like what it was originally but different, and the inside, although muddy, is padded and softer and must have been made to do a specific job. Around the edge the teeth are sharp and jagged as once upon a time it had gripped the bottle top and been very useful, but now if you are not careful the teeth could cut you. What you reckon Fred, do you recognise this bottle top".

There was quite a long pause, and then he took the object back from me.

"Yeah, I recognise this object. It's had its day, it's done its deed and it's lost its shine, it's a bit sad really isn't it? I can see what you're doing Richard, and I get it up to a point. It is a bit of a mirror, it's not what I meant it to be – I meant it to be bit of a laugh, but now it feels uncomfortable, like I've been unmasked".

"Dear Fred, this bottle top might in fact be showing you something really positive about yourself. Can you think of any way it could be helpful? This isn't a game to just make you feel bad – that is the last thing I want, and of course it is uncomfortable coming out of denial, making the decision to become visible, and I think unconsciously that is exactly what has happened today. Unconsciously you have shown us a part of yourself that you might not have had the words or understanding to be able to express consciously. I take this process very seriously, as I think it's an extraordinary route to discovery and I think the word you use is quite correct: you picked up a mirror."

At this point somebody else in the group picked up the object and was polishing it and cleaning it and pointing out that underneath the dirt it was still a shiny object and when he put it on his chest and showed it off as a medal, everybody clapped.

Fred took the bottle top back and held it more carefully this time and he now looked thoughtful and tearful, and said:

"How lonely it is being cast out, not having a purpose, being downtrodden and thinking you're not wanted. I can't quite put my finger on it, but I feel a sort of change or transformation taking place. There is some other meaning to this I can't quite get it yet, and 'medal' sounds about right. I feel like I have been on the frontline, I have been having to fight to survive. I did feel like a veteran that nobody wanted, and as I say that feels different now but I can't quite get it and I look forward to hearing about all your objects and maybe that will help. Thanks Richard."

"Thanks Fred, it takes courage to come out of hiding and there is risk involved. You are not alone in this, the process that has just happened will also be a mirror for somebody else. I don't believe it's just chance that the five of us are here sharing this together. When I introduced this exercise to you, I said there would be an object in the woods waiting for you."

13

Under Way

Under way: A vessel that is moving under control; that is, not at anchor, or made fast to the shore or aground or adrift.

IT WAS A beautiful sunny spring day, with scudding clouds over a blue sky, and a white flecked ultramarine and green sea, with enough wind to keep us cruising along the south coast of Cornwall. I found myself sitting next to Jane, up on the bows of *Physis*.

It was day three of a 4-day session with four women. Jane was one of the participants, a lively and enthusiastic member of the group in her early 20s. With a history of multiple drug abuse, and with sexually and physically abusive partners, she had been in a treatment centre for two months.

The night before in our therapy process group another member of the group had started talking about an event where she had been raped; this was quite a session as it triggered memories for other members of the group. Jane was unusually quiet and didn't partake much in that session.

She appeared to be distant and quite remote at breakfast the next day, and most of the morning she was also extremely quiet. We had been sailing gently up the coast and we had all been sitting at the stern of the boat in the cockpit, sharing our thoughts and generally gossiping and enjoying the ride. At some point Jane had gone up to sit at the bows on her own. It was not particularly unusual for someone to find peace and quiet up there, as it was a beautiful spot to sit and watch the world go by.

After half an hour I decided to go up and check if she was alright and sat at a slight angle to her so that I could observe her face and body language. We were quiet together for a long while, and I had the sense that she was quite distressed. She was looking ahead, and her eyes were ceaselessly moving left and right, watching the world go by. I find that I can sit in such a place and just let my eyes relax and scan ahead. I would be naturally scanning for any little variation in this simple and relaxed environment, maybe a boat on the horizon, a fleck of white water on a wave, a bird or a cloud.

After a while I turned to her and remarked that it was unusual for her to be so quiet and withdrawn. There was quite a long pause. She turned to me and said, *"It's very beautiful here but it's very difficult right now, I'm feeling quite shitty, really quite unbearable emotionally and physically."*

"Okay and what's going on?"

Again, there was a long pause before she turned to me and said: *"This is the anniversary of a multiple rape that happened to me when I was 14."*

Again, I just waited and let her set the pace. *"Since the group last night, a lot of emotions got triggered and I am having flashbacks even though it happened nine years ago."*

"So, what's it like telling me?" Tears were running down her face. *"You know, Richard, this is the first time I have told anybody. Never told anybody in treatment, never told anybody when it happened. This is the first time you know. It's such a relief and I feel so sad and angry."*

I thanked her for telling me and told her that it was important to let it out. After all, grief and anger sounded understandable reactions to me under the circumstances. Again, quite a long pause.

"Not just the first time telling anybody; it's also the first time I've been able to stay with this horror, all these jumbled up emotions. All morning I wanted to get away from everybody, get off my head, do anything, cut myself, anything not to feel the shit, but here I am sitting on my own, with you next to me, still feeling crap. It's weird and it's sort of good as well in a way – I can feel something fundamental shifting and changing."

"That sounds pretty normal, as it sounds like it's the first time you have given yourself a chance to process this appalling event. It takes real courage to just sit here and let yourself be in it. I'm here next to you and I hear you."

The conversation went on something like that and we stayed at the bows together for a little while and then returned to sit with the others in the cockpit. It didn't take long before the chatter and jokes started amongst the group, but Jane said she couldn't say much about what was going on for her – she would be able to say more in the group that evening.

During group process, Jane was extremely grateful and quite overwhelmed. They were able to share tears and show their solidarity. I pointed out to them all the importance of what Jane had experienced that day, not just for herself but for all of them. Sharing this with the group would be the beginning of a new life and, for Jane, the trauma of this memory would never be the same again.

As for me, I felt uplifted. Occasions such as this made all the hard work seem worthwhile. I understood that a powerful process had led to some form of transition and I was fascinated to know more about how this had come about. After watching her on the bows, I had a hunch that the secret of the process might be to do with EMDR, Eye Movement Desensitisation Reprocessing. I wanted to know more, so this was also the beginning of a new journey for me.

My wife Sue, an EMDR practitioner, gave me some useful information. She was convinced that Jane, quite unconsciously, had been practising the process of EMDR. We know from neuroscientists that, to process trauma, both left and right brain need to be engaged at the same time,[1] using bilateral stimulation (eye movement or taps).

Combining an Empathic Psychotherapeutic Relationship with sailing creates the best possible environment for stimulating an individual's latent natural organismic capacity (Physis) to regulate and process their here-and-now emotional experience BUT ALSO any archaic experience which may surface during the process.

Here was a crystal-clear example of this for me, and so exciting. I believed that this was what had happened for Jane. She had started the process by using rapid eye movement, scanning the horizon, scanning the environment around her, her eyes moving left and right, and then continuing the process with me, an empathic psychotherapist, who helped to put the experience into words. It was also interesting that she had managed to stay with these powerful and unpleasant emotions. As this had been the third day of a four-day session, I believe that over the previous days she had managed to enhance her resilience, which gave her the tenacity to stay with the pain. The strength she had gained by being at one with nature and in a positive environment had been crucial in the process.

Back home, I studied as much as I could about neuroscience and EMDR. I read that the vagus nerve originates in the brain stem and then exits the cranium at the base of the skull where the two sides divide into ventral and dorsal (front and back) components. Polyvagal Theory[2] describes the

---

1   (Schore, 1994). EMDR (Shapiro, 1989, 2012)

2   Polyvagal Theory: is a collection of evolutionary neuroscientific and psychological claims pertaining to the role of the vagus nerve in a emotion regulation social connection, and fear responses. Konorski J, in Livingston RB, 1966, *Brain mechanisms in conditioning and learning. Neurosciences Research Program Bulletin.* (4)(3): 349

autonomic nervous system as having 3 subdivisions that relate to social behaviour and connection.

The frontal cortex section of the brain controls our ability to self-soothe, to regulate emotions, be relational and appraise threat. It also controls non-verbal empathy, when we resonate without words, and models the brain path for a return to calm. Our prefrontal cortex gives us wisdom, mind sight, empathy and our soul. It is the part of our brain that makes us human.

When we use words to name experience, we also activate the prefrontal cortex and begin to calm the amygdala (chimp) limbic system. With the chimp brain unregulated, the central brain will make assessments on fight, flight, freeze, or appease. There is no "past," there is only right now, the ever-present. High activity in the amygdala part of the brain often suggests addictive behaviour.

Now to the reptilian brain. The dorsal (back) part of the brain will register threat, but there is no here and now, only archaic (ancient) memory. The reptilian 'knows' how to *be* in the natural environment (body-sensing, reptilian experience). It is thought by some that this part of the brain is where trauma and shame may be lodged. Further reading suggested to me that we also have a relationship to nature which is primitive, and our disconnection from nature therefore has consequences.

This was so relevant to activities on the boat, and this part of the jigsaw really began to fall into place, whether it is being, doing, thinking, or any combination, as when helming by compass, and often then when a participant is repeatedly making a variety of mistakes. I could see now that there is an interruption to the natural flow within the brain, and I now had a tool to analyse this. The trauma had become visible, understandable and logical, here in this weird activity of helming and thinking. Psychological corrections can be made, not just in behaviour, but in the creation of new neural pathways. Working with nature, and within an empathic relationship, neural damage can be repaired.

Jane had been experiencing non-verbal empathy in her relationship to the environment and nature around her. When we resonate without words, the brain path is modelled for a return to calm, and again creates new neural pathways. When words are used to name experience and feelings, which had been the next step for Jane, her prefrontal cortex had been activated and began to calm her chimp brain – the part that wanted to cut herself or get out of her head. The next stage of the process was for her brain's energy to find some form of freedom and get some sort of insight, mind sight, be creative again instead of controlled by her overwhelming feelings caused by the trauma. I came to understand that two forms of empathic relationship were here: Jane's relationship with nature, and with me, with both supporting the growth of new neural connections between the prefrontal cortex and the chimp brain.

I felt that I had been privileged to observe a unique and significant process that not just helped Jane but set me upon a course that I now travelled willingly. I learned from neuro-scientific research that experience can actually change both the brain's physical structure (anatomy) and its functional organisation (psychology) after development. The more recent research showed how the brain can, and does, change in response to hitherto unsuspected stimuli.

Here was a whole new world opening up for me of what experiential education was about, much deeper than just increasing awareness, improving our self-confidence and self-esteem.

The eighth International Adventure Therapy Conference was due in June of the following year in Denver, USA. I prepared my abstract, writing up a presentation and workshop, demonstrating how working with nature can be beneficial. A process of not just repairing psychological and emotional damage, but from my understanding of what I had witnessed, through neuroplasticity the brain can help to repair itself.

Neuroplasticity, also known as brain plasticity,[3] refers to changes in neural pathways and synapses due to changes in behaviour, environment, neural processes, thinking, emotions, and changes resulting from bodily injury. Neuroplasticity has replaced the formerly held theory that the brain is a physiologically static organ and explores how the brain changes throughout life.

I realised that I was on the cutting edge, exploring an area in this field (or ocean) of knowledge that was not well researched. Our disassociation and disconnection from nature was having a profound effect on us individually and geopolitically. I had an instinctive sense that there was some shame that we have become distanced from nature, and that this disconnection is traumatic. There is an emotional bond with nature, and human consciousness yearns for this connection – to be reconnected. That deep resonance can be recognised in the face of someone sitting on a mountain top, or on a clifftop watching the sea.

Evolution has affected the human mind. Neuropsychologists[4] hold that humankind's mind comes from nature and does not function apart from nature. The whole brain includes functions of both hemispheres of

---

3   Rodale Tudor K, Neopsyche chapter in Hargaden & Sills eds, 2002.
4   Ashbrook (2003) a neuropsychologist, believes that humankind's whole mind comes out of nature.

the "new brain," but is also influenced by the symbolic and subconscious activity of the "old brain" with its somatic and environmental roots. The old mammalian (reptilian) brain contains the biological root of human bonding with nature, a bonding that enabled the human species to survive for 3 million years. As the human brain and a sense of kinship evolved together, empathic caring marks the most striking change in evolutionary adaptation. This need for empathic caring is evidenced in people's need and desire for love and emotional bonding—with humans as well as nature. The desired emotional bond with nature that the human consciousness yearns for and needs is left unfulfilled. Roszak (1995) believed that humans *do* have an inner desire to care for the planet.

I wanted to share what had happened to Jane and the whole subsequent process with other adventure therapists at the Denver conference. I was excited and really interested to hear what other people would make of it. I did not realise it, but there would be profound consequences for myself. Being there at that specific time brought together a structure of beliefs and some misunderstandings that I could no longer ignore; this internal conflict must have been simmering in my unconscious for some time.

During the conference I attended several lectures and workshops, of which two stand out in my mind as game-changers for me. On arrival, and as I was choosing which lectures and workshops to attend, I was heartened to see that neuroplasticity was a buzzword. It was the new influence, the new understanding, and consequently I really thought I had something to offer. It was a relief to me because I often felt I was in a vacuum living and working in Cornwall. Seven months of the year I was sailing with groups and either preparing, recovering or managing sessions. I had little time left to study and meet like-minded people in what seem like faraway places. My winters were generally spent fundraising and analysing and writing up the work of the previous seven months.

An Israeli therapist from Gaza who I greatly respect gave a lecture that left me dumbfounded and in tears. She was describing how she took a group out into the desert for a week to find their stress points and for the group to determine how to resource themselves to continue when they considered they had reached their limits. She described an experience when she could no longer carry her backpack. She felt as though she was carrying the whole world on her back and became confused and angry. She knew she had the capacity to continue but suddenly her body was giving out. She described the mental anguish and her sense of betrayal that she had to ask for help. She was the leader, the mentor, she should not have been the feeble one who struggled and gave up.

I really recognised this process as I had felt I was carrying the whole world on *my* back, carrying the group, the charity, everybody's trauma, stress and strain. Compared to the stress of finding funding for the charity to continue, and that of the preparatory work and organising the sessions, preparing the clients and participants was peanuts. Right there, in that lecture theatre, I could hear a voice in my head saying, *"I can't carry on, I can't do this any longer, I'm so alone, and nobody can help me"*. I was sitting there, sensing this great weight on my back and the tears started streaming down my face. When I saw the lecturer look at me and our eyes met, I knew I could dig deep to find the courage to carry on, but that I needed help. I felt shame and grief and loneliness; this lecture had disrobed me, uncovered me and bared my soul. This place felt so familiar – as the starting place of my recovery. I needed help, I could no longer do this on my own, but what was it that I could not do on my own?

I did talk to other group leaders during the next few days, and I came to the conclusion that I was burning out and probably reaching my limit. I needed to do something about it for my own health and, of course, those who were dependent upon me.

The other lecture which moved me greatly was given by two scientists who had recently been attending a conference in Stockholm about the climate emergency. This was the first time I had heard this term, although I had been aware since 1967 that we were likely to be reaching the limits to our growth as the human population of this planet. The information was stark and frightening. I became aware that we have very nearly reached the point where global warming and our possible extinction is inevitable – it is almost beyond healing and there is no going back. I recognised very quickly and understood that our divorce from nature and our addiction as consumers is going to kill us. When had I heard that before? Which 12-Step meeting, which addiction centre residential had I been to, how long had I been privy to this information and not done anything about it? I felt more grief, anger and despair.

I didn't fully comprehend how much I had been affected by this conference, but I knew that it was different from all the others. I was yet to realise the true significance of the effect on me of this combination of information and awareness. I took a week off after the conference and went white-water rafting in the Rockies. It was exciting, but I also had a sense of being lost and driven. The sensation of being thrown down the river with minimal control was similar to the emotions I was going through when thinking about Sailaday OK.

I understood I needed to make changes, personal changes, and changes to the structure of Sailaday. There was also a sense of something having cracked, as if a seismic change was under way, even though I couldn't quite grasp it. I couldn't see it but I could feel the tremors.

14

Up Shit Creek
Without a Paddle

Up shit creek without a paddle: This referred to trying
to get down Deptford canal towards the Isle of Dogs, but
due to the canal being silted up your oar is stuck – you
can't go backwards and you can't go forwards.

THE AUTUMN OF 2015 was a hectic time as I worked with the Sailaday OK
trustees to get our charity and ship in good order. I worked hard with the
Chair and other trustees to get all our charitable frameworks in good order.
This involved rewriting policy documents to cover equal opportunities,
health and safety, complaints procedure, volunteer management, vulnerable
beneficiaries, and conflict of interests. We also put in place an investment
policy ready for if and when we decided to open a trading company. All this
took a great deal of time and effort and I was grateful for the support as it
gave me space to start planning for the future.

I was full of ideas and quite keyed up for the future, but at the same time
aware of my limitations. I began to look at the possibilities of employing a
skipper and purchasing a larger sailing yacht, planning to fulfil the role of
CEO and be the primary therapist.

As we were heading towards the end of the 2015 sailing season I found
myself spending time making notes and writing up ideas for developing
a programme for a larger and fuller funding application. At the end of
each season, between October and January, I was required to fulfil my
commitments to our funders and write up reports and analyses of how

Sailaday had performed in the previous year. Our records for the Big Lottery were exquisite. We had always gone above and beyond our commitments, and we achieved better outcomes and worked with more participants than planned. So, this was a good time to take stock, particularly as we had two years to complete a new application.

In the middle of December, I received a phone call from Buckingham Palace asking me if I would accept an award of the British Empire Medal if I was offered it. I was told not to tell anybody and wait for the announcement in January 2016.

I put out the following press release that January.

Release 2016 From Richard Lannowe Hall BEM March 6th

Saturday March 28th from 5.30pm to 7.30pm Richard Lannowe Hall will host his BEM Award Ceremony. The ceremony will be conducted by Colonel Bolitho, Lord-Lieutenant of Cornwall, accompanied by Cllr John Wood, Chairman, Cornwall Council, at The Eco Park, The Meeting Room, Mount Pleasant Eco Park, Chapel Hill, Porthtowan, Cornwall TR4 8HL

The Award is 'for services to adventure therapy and addiction services in the south west UK.' This was part of the Order of the British Empire and awarded for either Meritorious Service or for 'Gallantry'.

This is a remarkable and inspiring story, as Richard suffered 25 years of multiple drugs and alcohol abuse and drew on his experiences of recovery to create this unique and successful charity.

Richard says, "I feel honoured to receive this recognition of my work with Sailaday OK and grateful for the nomination and support of our brilliant team. I trust that this achievement will give hope and inspiration to all others who have also suffered/suffer from addictions, abuse and trauma. I am pleased that Sailaday Ok is also receiving this exposure and this will help us in the development of the marine adventure therapy charity and our search for a Patron."

There will be cream teas supplied by the very supportive Eco Park team, and music by Steve Slimm and a good photo opportunity.

It was wonderful to feel recognised for what I and the charity had achieved, and I came to realise that this process had started some two years before the announcement of the award. I remembered being asked some personal questions by the Chair of the board of trustees and at the time had wondered why, but I soon forgot about it. There had been quite a lengthy process of assessing the value of the charity and making absolutely sure that there were no skeletons in any cupboards.

The BEM dates back to our colonial past. Originally it was awarded to people of the British Empire who had demonstrated great courage, and for a short while I considered declining the award as I wasn't entirely happy with the idea of being connected to our colonial past. However, I thought to myself, *"If Mick Jagger can accept that, so can I!"* At the time, it didn't occur to me that the most important aspect of my acceptance might be that it could give hope to those who are hopeless and can see no future or value in their lives. *"If Richard can do that, so can I!"*

There were a number of statements taken from professionals and our clients, mainly the managers of the residential centres we worked with. The Chair had also managed to contact some participants, including several who claimed that not only had I dramatically changed their lives, but also probably saved their lives.

I was being highly honoured for what I had achieved and created and felt that this was the cream on the top of the cake. I saw the award as a real stimulus for the charity and thought that it would help us bring in the funding we needed, attract the patron we wanted, and that fame and glory were on the way. However, it wasn't long before that bubble burst.

Two years earlier I had been at the Czechoslovakia conference and had come away thinking that there was a basic flaw with Sailaday OK. I suspect that I had known it for a while but hadn't really wanted to face it or felt confident enough to voice it. Sailaday OK was a one-man band – it was Richard Lannowe Hall. Each of the trustees of course had a specific role to play, maybe in the role of Chair, someone to handle all the promotional material and printing, another to have been a participant on a sailing therapy session and hence give valuable feedback. We also needed an accountant, a treasurer and a secretary, but there was nobody who could share the burden of the sailing sessions, the role of being the skipper, the therapist and everything else that this entailed. It was down to me to handle the intakes, the presentations and evaluations, with only some help available for documenting and analysing these. There was little room or energy left for development and progress, and if anything happened to me the charity would undoubtedly fold. I realised that this was not a healthy state of affairs, although I understand now how it had come about. The development of the charity had been fairly organic but, when I look back on it, there must have been a fair bit of ego involved.

Over the next couple of years this flaw increasingly bothered me and I began to feel stressed and overwhelmed. I discussed the problem with the trustees and friends and family, but there seemed to be no way out of the shit creek we had sailed into. This situation had developed directly out of my experience of recovery from my various addictions and so how was I going to find somebody with a similar history as well as someone having a passion and deep understanding of sailing? Who on earth could we actively collaborate with, and how was I going to learn to delegate?

To comply with the criteria of many of the grant-funding bodies, one of the big buzzwords was 'collaboration'. With whom could I collaborate? Another sailing organisation, another adventure therapy organisation; to be honest my mind went blank. Prospective funders tried to help with suggestions to tick the right boxes – "Why don't you work with paraplegics?" "Why don't you work with young children?" "Why don't you give up residential work?" Nothing they suggested was right for Sailaday OK.

Being awarded the BEM was wonderful recognition of what I had achieved, but also seemed to highlight our weakness, our Achilles' heel.

It took me two years of gnawing at this bone before I found any clarity. I had been blind to the fact that I had not followed my own advice that "when the wind changes, I need to change course". Trying to maintain the same course will most likely lead you into danger, distress and failure. Some of the clarity had come about while I was at the Denver conference.

Two years after the Czechoslovakia conference, I was invited to Denver USA to deliver a lecture and a workshop. I had become increasingly interested in neuroscience and understanding that addiction serves to keep raw, unprocessed emotional experience out of awareness because of an inability to process it, to feel it through, to come to terms with what has happened. Unfortunately, people who are traumatised are not only unable to process the experience which afflicted them in the first place but frequently have been unable to process many subsequent life events, "resulting in a multiple pile-up of emotional experience which has never been expressed." (Parker Hall, 2008)

My visit to Denver USA had been critical, due to those particularly outstanding and impactful lectures and workshops, which I referred to in the previous chapter. This effect on me had been unexpected and extremely emotional.

As mentioned, I had been particularly emotionally affected at that conference by the presentation given by the Israeli therapist. She recounted how she had tried to be Superwoman as she struggled to carry and lead her charity and groups in a gruelling and challenging environment. She had continued until she collapsed; the pressure and stress of leadership had become unbearably heavy, and her resources had been sucked dry. I had totally identified with this scenario. I felt I was carrying the weight of the world on my shoulders; I needed help, as I couldn't carry it any longer on my own. The Israeli therapist had described how she had finally asked all the members of her group to help share the load so she could walk for a while without the pack and have time to recover. This had proved to be a significant lesson for me – it gave me permission not to be Superman. I now had to find a way of putting down the burden, by sharing it and redesigning the structure of Sailaday.

I have also touched on the other presentation that had resonated with me, describing the ecological nightmare we are facing on a global scale, in which the presenter gave an analysis of how we have arrived at this dire situation. What he described and put into words were thoughts and fluctuating wisps of ideas that had been haunting me for some time, but I had not been able to gather them together as clearly as he did. I do not have scientific information about global warming at my fingertips, but I believe I understand how we have become disconnected from nature.

My history of being involved with Scouts, Duke of Edinburgh Awards and other outdoor pursuits had led me towards adventure therapy and outdoor education. I understand that the use of the wilderness and nature as a part of the healing process and traditional rites of passage into adulthood can be traced back in history to many cultures.

Our industrial accomplishments are simply leading us deeper into a meaningless world. All our inventions and our medicinal formulas only serve to keep at bay the deep anxieties to which we are now subject, and our massive military expenditure cannot keep us secure. We are frightened, both personally and nationally, and in our communities, by the least threat to life or security. We seek protection through ever greater control over other humans and over the natural world that we inhabit. Yet adequate security has always eluded us. We are threatened, as never before, by natural elements such as the atmosphere, the water, the soil, and the various living forms that we have abused. We are threatened by the enemies we have made with the very efforts that we have made toward national security. We do not know how to relate to the natural world, and we are uncertain in our relations with the human world.

In my reading, I came to explore and understand how nature-based evolution has affected the human mind. Ashbrook (2003), a neuropsychologist, believes that humankind's whole mind comes out of nature and does not function apart from nature. The old mammalian (reptilian) brain contains the biological root of human bonding with nature, a bonding that enabled the human species to survive for 3 million years. As the human brain and a sense of kinship evolved together, empathic caring marks the most striking change in evolutionary adaptation. The desired emotional bond with nature that the human consciousness yearns for and needs is left unfulfilled.

The industrial-commercial world can go no further. It has achieved its goal. It dominates the planet. We have reached the limits of growth.[1]

Society is forever erecting barriers between its citizens and the inner/ outer wilderness. On the outer side, we have our air-conditioned houses and automobiles, gated communities and indoor malls, fences and animal control officers, dams and virtual realities. On the inner side, we're offered prescribed 'mood enhancers', alcohol, and street drugs; consumerism and dozens of other soul-numbing addictions; mobile phones, fundamentalisms, transcendentalisms, and other escapisms; rigid belief systems as to what is "good" and what is "bad"; who are 'The Right' and who are 'The Left' and belief systems that God or some other paternal figure will watch over us and protect our delicate risk-free lives. We have at our fingertips greater and faster forms of communication and access to Internet information but, lacking in knowledge, we have become even more divorced from nature, from our natural yearning to connect with our source, our wilding, our source of knowledge, wisdom and truth.

I came to understand that the gift I have to give is not an attempt to save the world, as that undertaking would be merely ego based. My misunderstanding of the use of this gift would likely lead only to frustration and pain. However, I came to see that what I could offer – my true self – is the best I can do, giving love as my service. I read somewhere that love is all the world needs. By consciously honouring my grief, our universal grief and trauma of disconnection, I am taking the first step towards personal fulfilment. I thought I was already on course, but I needed to trim the sails in order to return to my true nature and make this emotional bond with nature that I and, I believe, all humanity's consciousness yearn too for this connection.

---

1   Roszak (1995, p. 7) 1992, his book, *The Voice of the Earth*

The consequence of these thoughts was doubt and disenchantment with adventure therapy. I felt that it could be part of the outmoded way of using nature to further our ends and desires. I began to think that I could not just go out there and take people with me to have an experience in nature and not give anything back – it had to be reciprocal. I came to understand that I needed to move away from adventure therapy and towards eco-therapy.[2] This could be seen as a subtle difference, but these insights, thoughts and ideas changed fundamentally my understanding of my relationship with nature. I came to understand that nature is not just something outside of me, out there in the wild in the green or blue gym, but something far more intrinsic – I *am* nature.[3]

For centuries we have looked on nature and the natural environment as something to use for our benefit and I developed an increasing anxiety that I had been doing something similar with adventure therapy, and so, at the very least, I was not happy with continuing in that vein.

By the end of that Denver conference, I felt I had been well fed, and had become excited about the future and willing to make some of these changes. Firstly, however, I gave myself a few days of R&R in the Rockies – they really are such a gigantic range of mountains. I was in awe of the size of the USA; I had thought that crossing the Atlantic was a long journey, but I hadn't realised that flying from Newark to Denver would take nearly the same amount of time – incredible.

I hired a car and drove into the Rockies and booked myself a couple of sessions of white-water rafting. The tops of the mountains were still covered in snow and it was weird driving along the motorway and being passed by cars with snowboards and skis on the roof racks, even though it was mid-July and it was hot. The mountain waterways were full of extremely cold water, moving at a terrifying pace. The river we were to raft down had a huge amount of very white water, with anything up to 10-foot drops. I loved it and was pleased to be immersed in water again even though we were locked within an enormous mountain range. There would be stretches of river we raced down and then suddenly there would be calm spots and places to take a breath. Our group was well managed and was led by an experienced rafter who told us what to do and how to do it, generating plenty of adrenalin and

---

2   Eco-psychology or eco-therapy is a therapeutic technique and ideology that attempts to treat people psychologically by bringing them spiritually closer to nature. Ecopsychologists try to develop beneficial emotional bonds with nature and their thinking is very much about the bad connections with the environment may be partially behind many psychological problems.

3   "I *am* nature". Andy Goldworthy, environmentalist and sculptor 1989, *Common Ground* ISBN 1-870364-07-

group bonding, and now I had the T-shirt to go with it. The experience felt like a metaphor for the previous 10 years of my life.

This had been an enjoyable intermission and change of scenery and I came back to the UK refreshed and ready to enact the changes I had planned. We had one year left of the five years of funding from Big Lottery and it was time to do some planning ahead. As soon as I got back, I started the process of reassessing and rethinking the structure and the mission statement for Sailaday OK. We were already in the process of making applications for funding, however, without much success so far.

All those involved with Sailaday OK became involved in a lengthy process of navel-gazing, rethinking, analysing what we were, what we did, and how we did it – nothing less than completely redefining our brand. The first step was to get some of our groundwork solid: rewrite our mission statement, which felt out of date, and some of our more formal policy documents. It was exhausting and, it took the wind out of my sails. Too much formal form filling and documenting.

I also spent some of that autumn thinking about and looking for new clients, preparing ourselves for the end of the funding we were receiving from the Big Lottery. We had a two-year window in which to make the application for the funding we wanted and to create the programme we thought we could achieve.

New clients included young people, and in particular young people who had been affected by their carer's addictions. The plan was that these would be interactive sessions with primary carers and young persons, as I wanted to work with them together.

I also wanted to work more with military veterans. Those who have retired from military service and are quite likely to have experienced combat and been negatively affected by it. Whenever we'd had a veteran within another group, they had always found the sessions extremely therapeutic. One of the things I learned from them was that when they were together as veterans in their supportive groups they could just about manage, but as soon as they started to integrate with their families, things would go wrong. So, I wanted to work with the veterans *and* their families – partners and children.

I began to write up some programmes and managed to obtain some start-up funding, with some good support from the press and caring agencies. However, there was a highly negative response from charities that worked with veterans. Help for Heroes were quite aggressive in telling me that psychotherapy of the sort I was offering didn't really help people suffering from trauma and they had perfectly good institutions themselves. However, I learned later that the Help for Heroes charity at that time did not work with veterans, only with those still in the military. I was shocked at the lack of support that veterans could get, particularly if it also involved their families. The highest suicide rate in UK is amongst veterans. This was tragic and upsetting and I found it hard to break through the wall of resistance.

Addaction, however, were extremely supportive, helpful and interested in getting our young people's programme up and running. That autumn we ran our first trial sessions – one-day sessions with three children and a carer who they were familiar with. The feedback was great, and I was looking forward to developing this in the following year. I even had the idea that if we had the right equipment, maybe a large inflatable hard-rib dinghy, we could run some winter programmes.

Another great buzzword from funding agencies is 'self-sufficiency', so we created a trading company – Sailaday Eco – with the intention of creating our own income and aiming towards self-sufficiency sometime in the future. It takes a great deal of money to run a boat, and to pay professionals, so quite how working with people with no money was going to make us self-sufficient wasn't a question we could really answer at that time. It was a sort of vague hope.

However, it being close to my heart, I created Sailaday Eco primarily to cater for professionals, eco-psychologists and those working in the eco-therapy field, as these would all be fee-paying clients. During 2016 we ran free trial sessions which generated brilliant feedback and plenty of enthusiasm, but that was as far as it went: Sailaday Eco never generated a single fee-paying client.

We relaunched Sailaday OK in spring 2016, with a new Charity Commission number and a new mission statement, which read:

- Reduce disadvantage and social exclusion by giving relief and rehabilitation to those recovering from addictions, abuse and trauma by the provision of therapeutic sailing and marine-based adventure.
- Educate therapists and skippers in the benefits of therapeutic sailing and marine-based adventure therapy by providing a structured training programme including supervised practice.

We were also going to extend our client base to include young people affected by their carers' addictions and develop our mentoring programme. All this was to try to placate our funders and cover all our bases. Prospective funders still found one reason or another to turn us down. I was getting exhausted, writing and rewriting a major application to the Big Lottery. They didn't seem to comprehend that Sailaday OK was a unique charity and how successful it had been. They suggested that there were too many other organisations providing the same opportunities and support. However, this was clearly not the case as, at that time, no residential sailing programmes working with this client group existed in the UK. They suggested that we collaborate, for example, with people near Falmouth who took paraplegic people sailing. The fact that I hadn't got a clue how to work with paraplegics and our boat was nowhere near suitable didn't seem to make any impression on Big Lottery. Even though our results were fantastic and dependent on being residential, they were offering funding for non-residential groups. It was all very depressing.

There seemed to be a similar story in the wider addiction therapy world, in that Government was not supporting long-term residential units. They wanted quick fixes, which, to me, are a complete waste of time. My personal experience, reinforced by my experience of working with Sailaday's clients, had been that people needed at least two years of continued therapeutic support.

I approached agencies to help us with our funding applications and to gain some advice on how we could promote ourselves more effectively. Feedback from those we did approach was often that our "*BRAND* was not clear." The fact was that we could not afford the fees of most of these agencies. It was Catch 22 – without external funding, we didn't have the finance to pay hundreds of pounds an hour to help us in our applications. Consequently, the big charities could achieve professional support and could go to workshops and weekend retreats offered to CEOs and those involved in funding applications. Sailaday OK could not.

We couldn't even afford the train fares to get to some of the conferences, and when I suggested that the bigger charities help subsidise the smaller charities, I was met with a barrage of indifference at best and derision at worst. The pot of gold for charities was getting smaller, and the big boys were clearly not in the sharing business.

The trustees, and all involved with Sailaday, attended two lengthy all-day sessions to define the charity's 'brand'. I will always remember these workshops, which proved to be a fascinating process. Although tiring, they were stimulating, and I really enjoyed the experience of being so closely involved with all the trustees. It was the first time we had all come together to work through these difficulties. We finally arrived at an inclusive term – 'Quantum Recovery', which represented significant differences in approach, leading to transformation.

The image that comes to mind now is that of a fish just landed on the deck of the boat, thrashing around gasping for air, not quite understanding why the oxygen was in fact killing it – it was dying however much thrashing it did. The clear metaphor being that the more I thrashed about, the closer I came to extinction.

15

Take Soundings

Take soundings: In suspected shallow waters, a crew member may have the task of repeatedly throwing into the water a lead line – a piece of lead tied to a string knotted at every fathom, for the purpose of estimating the depth of the sea. This saying is the nautical equivalent of "Take the lay of the land": see how things are going, or see what people think about a proposed course of action.

Quantum Recovery

I WAS READING different material and talking to different people about working with nature, and my dream was subtly changing. I was taking new soundings. For example, reading and researching the psychological benefits of experiencing nature. As far as I could find out, this was first posted in 1989 by Kaplan, who introduced the idea that nature, in all its complexity and beauty, "...elicits deep-seated and automatic responses by individuals in the absence of extensive information processing". Theodore Roszak also believes that there is recovery, and that restoration derives from the reduction of stimulus and arousal due to nature's calming effect, which "... elicits positively toned emotional states and blocks out negatively toned feelings". Nature removes individuals from their accustomed culture and surrounds them with a natural world that is calming and nurturing. The impact this has on emotional states and thought processes can be positive and restorative.

Sailaday OK had designed a therapeutic model to support recovering addicts in reconnecting, to make that personal, environmental and possibly spiritual connection, and to recover. We came to understand participants could not do this on their own. Recovery needs to be in relationship not just to nature but also to other people. The marine environment – the blue gym – for me, had all the elements that Kaplan describes. This was the space where I found my inspiration and where I experienced tranquillity and nurturing, even when it was unpredictable, grey and apparently unfriendly. I was never judged by this environment; it was out there that I found love.

Through our trustees' collaborative process of navel-gazing and attempts to analyse our 'brand' we came to the conclusion that when we offered marine adventure therapy, it was a way to connect with the present, the crew and nature. This empathic connection to nature is an uplifting experience and helps people to make some "significant, spectacular steps, changes, and transformation and consequently achieve **quantum recovery**."

At this time, we added to our arsenal of promotional material a new strapline that could be added to emails, leaflets etc., or most commonly, as a small sticker, which had this motto on it:

SAILADAY OK GIVES YOU A GREAT CONNECTION, but there is NO WIFI at sea!!

Reading the work of Bruce Alexander, Professor of Psychology in Vancouver,[1] and studying his experiments and writings, I came to understand the rationale that recovery from addictions cannot be done in isolation.

He writes that there are strong chemical hooks in drugs, capable of creating a craving – a need for the chemical – within only twenty-one days' usage. A user can then be in the grip of a ferocious craving. That is what **addiction** means. Alexander was party to simple experiments to define addiction. A rat would be placed in a cage, alone, with two water bottles. One was just water, but the other was water laced with heroin or cocaine. Almost every time, the rat would become obsessed with the drugged water and would come back again and again until the substance finally killed it.

In the 1970s, Professor Alexander noticed something odd about this experiment. What would happen, he wondered, if we tried this differently? He built Rat Park – a lush cage where the rats would have coloured balls, the best rat food, tunnels to scamper down and plenty of friends. The rats with such good lives didn't like the drugged water. They mostly shunned it, consuming less than a quarter of the drugs that the isolated rats used,

---

1   Bruce Alexander described his experiments *"Rat Park"*, Psychopharmacology journal in the 1970s and early '80s

and none of them died. However, all the rats that were alone and unhappy became heavy users and died. He re-ran earlier experiments where the rats were left alone and became compulsive users of the drugs and left them for 57 days. He then took them out of isolation and placed them in the happy Rat Park. He wanted to know if the state of addiction the isolated rats had succumbed to would be permanent. The results were striking. The rats did show signs of a few twitches of withdrawal, but they soon stopped their heavy use and went back to having a 'normal' life. Their happier life in Rat Park had saved them.

It became clear to me that the opposite of addiction is not sobriety, but human connection. So, we offered an environment specifically designed for our participants to make interpersonal, environmental and spiritual connections. This would be a safe, nurturing environment in which to recover from chemical addictions and consequently make changes to the underlying issues of abuse, trauma, and the underlying core belief that, *"I am a bad person, if you knew me, really knew me, you would be disgusted."*

One of the positive outcomes promoted by adventure therapy, and many other outdoor activities, is participants' ability to increase their confidence and self-esteem. However, I believe that confidence and self-esteem are not the same thing. Activities that can enhance confidence do not necessarily increase self-value, self-esteem, unless the individual is given therapeutic support to integrate and process the successful experience of an activity. I have found that they can, in some instances, experience even greater shame – *"If you really knew me!"; "The others are so much better than me!"; "See – I told you I'd be no good"*. The reduction of shame is necessary before self-esteem can be increased. Feelings of shame can be lessened with self-compassion and self-evaluation. However, I came to understand that being in relationship to someone or something is the route to the recovery of self. This cannot happen in isolation but can only happen by making a connection with Nature, as this relationship is undemanding and benign and became the route I was exploring.

During all my time working as skipper/therapist with the charity Sailaday OK, I collected information from evaluations and feedback from over 500 participants. These indicated that all the participants had experienced trauma and the consequential behaviour difficulties of all forms of addiction. Those addictions covered a wide spectrum: chemical (drugs and alcohol), gambling, work, sex, co-dependency and eating disorders. We built a therapy model that was intended to work with the underlying issues and not just with ways to manage the symptoms. On the surface you see the visible

– the negative behaviours. The trauma and underlying shame can usually be found in the next layer down.

Shame is a painful social emotion, which may stem from voluntary action or simply self-regard. No action by the shamed being is required: simply existing is enough. Both the comparison and standards are enabled by socialisation. Though usually considered an emotion, shame may also variously be considered an effect, cognition, state of being, or condition.

Psychoanalyst Helen B. Lewis[2] argued that... "The experience of shame is directly about the self, which is the focus of evaluation. In guilt, the self is not the central object of negative evaluation, but rather the thing done is the focus." Similarly, Fossum and Mason[3] say in their book *Facing Shame* that... "While guilt is a painful feeling of regret and responsibility for one's actions, shame is a crippling and painful feeling about oneself as a person."

Gershen Kaufman[4] summed up many of the consequences of shame in one paragraph of his book on the psychology of shame. "Shame is important because no other effect is more disturbing to the self, none more central for the sense of identity. In the context of normal development, shame is the source of low self-esteem, diminished self-image, poor self-concept, and deficient body-image. Shame itself produces self-doubt and disrupts both security and confidence. It can become an impediment to the experience of belonging and to shared intimacy... It is the experiential ground from which conscience and identity inevitably evolve. In the context of pathological development, shame is central to the emergence of alienation, loneliness, inferiority and perfectionism. It plays a central role in many psychological disorders as well, including depression, paranoia, addiction, and borderline conditions. Sexual disorders and many eating disorders are largely disorders of shame. Both physical abuse and sexual abuse also significantly involve shame."

Confidence and self-esteem are not the same thing, although they are often linked. Confidence is the term we use to describe how we feel about our ability to perform roles, functions and tasks; it's about what we **do**. Self-esteem is how we feel about ourselves, the way we look, the way we think – whether we feel worthy or valued, it's about who we **are** – our being.

People with low self-esteem often suffer from low levels of confidence, but people with good self-esteem can also have low confidence. It is also perfectly possible for people with low self-esteem to appear confident in some areas. These differences can be better understood if you start to take into account personality differences in particular around the narcissistic

2 Helen B Lewis; *Shame and Guilt in Neurosis*, ISBN, 978-0823 6075
3 Fossum and Mason *Facing Shame- Families in Recovery* ISBN 978- 0393305813
4 Gershen Kaufman. *The Psychology of Shame* ISBN 9780826166722

or borderline personality. Confidence includes knowing what to do when mistakes come to light and therefore is also about choices, problem-solving and decision-making. The common feature of the chemically addicted person is an inability to take responsibility to understand consequences. I believe you need a certain level of self-awareness and a sense of self-value to be responsible.

The many practitioners of adventure therapy talk about the increase in the participant's resilience, which can often be defined as an individual's ability to adapt, change and to face adverse conditions. My understanding of resilience is that it gives the owner an ability to bear the unbearable. In our previous chapter Jane had enough resilience to go and sit in the bows and bear the unbearable. However, there are many adventure therapy practitioners who promote the idea that they can build self-confidence and self-esteem, as if they are just small variations of the same thing. They are not.

So, I had to define self-esteem, and I concluded that it is about one's BEING, one's value. You may think of it as your inner voice – the voice that tells you whether you are good enough to do or achieve something. Self-esteem is about how we value ourselves, our perception and beliefs in who we are and, consequently, what we are capable of. Our self-esteem can be misaligned with other people's perception of who we are. In sociology and psychology, self-esteem reflects a person's overall subjective emotional evaluation of his or her own worth. It is a judgment of oneself as well as an attitude toward the self. This results in a state of lovelessness – "I am unlovable".

I believe that self-esteem may, in fact, be one of the most essential core self-evaluation dimensions because it is the overall value one feels about oneself as a person. Self-esteem is important because it shows us how we view the way we are and the sense of our personal value. Thus, it affects the way we are and act in the world and our view of others in that world, how we are related to and relate to others.

Carl Rogers (1902-1987), an advocate of humanistic psychology, theorised the origin of many people's problems to be that they despise themselves and consider themselves worthless and incapable of being loved. This is why Rogers believed in the importance of giving unconditional acceptance to a client, and when this was done it could improve the client's self-esteem. In his therapy sessions with clients, he offered positive regard no matter what. Indeed, the concept of self-esteem has been approached since then in humanistic psychology as an inalienable right for every person, summarised in the following sentence: "Every human being, with no exception, for the mere fact to be it, is worthy of unconditional respect of everybody else; he deserves to esteem himself and to be esteemed."

One of the most widely used instruments, the Rosenberg Self-Esteem Scale (RSES) (Rosenberg, 1965)[5] is a 10-item self-esteem scale of scores that requires participants to indicate their level of agreement with a series of statements about themselves. If a subject's answers demonstrate solid self-regard, the scale regards them as well-adjusted. If those answers reveal some inner shame, it considers them to be prone to social deviance.

When considering this we developed our own well-being assessment, with 10 questions being answered by tick boxes, with a measuring scale of 1 to 10 for each question. The participants were required to complete a Well Being Star questionnaire at the beginning and end of each session. Using this, I could measure their changes in attitude towards themselves and identify pertinent influences.

Over the years of working with these participants and coming to understand their feedback and evaluations which often speak of overcoming not only their ability to '*do*' things, but also a much more positive attitude towards themselves. When the participant recognised that he was "content by doing nothing", you came to recognise his sense of BEING. A preliminary step to increasing their self-worth is to come out of denial, come to know and recognise that they are suffering shame; revealing the monster that is sitting on their shoulder. To do this they have to turn round and face it, name it and feel it. This can be a painful experience and the opportune moment for this process to happen is fleeting. It is most likely to happen when the participant is expressing their doubts and insecurity, fears and innermost feelings of inadequacy, when he or she becomes vulnerable. This process cannot happen in isolation, and it doesn't come about automatically when participating in an outdoor/adventure/learning experience; but it *is* more likely to happen when contained by an empathic psychotherapeutic relationship.

I love the Brothers Grimm's story, *Rumpelstiltskin,*[6] from the *Children's and Household Tales* of 1812. The miller's daughter who had the capacity, the capability and self- confidence of spinning gold out of straw but didn't have the ability to name her abuser, her perpetrator, her jailer, until the last night. A spell had been put upon her at birth and she belonged to the imp, the demon within her, to Rumpelstiltskin. But in the morning she guessed Rumpelstiltskin's name. Having been named, he tore himself to bits in a rage and the miller's daughter was free. I really get the metaphor about

---

5 RSES (Rosenberg, 1965) is a 10-item self-esteem scale of scores Rosenberg M, 1965, Princeton University Press; the Rosenberg self-esteem scale is considered a reliable and valid quantitative tool for self-esteem assessment.

6 Karpman SB, 1968, *Fairy tales and script drama analysis, Transactional Analysis*, Bulletin, 7.

shame in this story – she named her shame, and in doing so she became free. And by the way, I am interested that Rumpelstiltskin experiences rage, which I believe is a symptom of shame.

Of course, what I am really interested in is what happened during her last night. What did she do differently from the previous nights to be able to recognise the demon and name the perpetrator? My thoughts, based on my own experiences, are about how she might have connected with a different part of herself, maybe stopped thinking and stopped guessing. Perhaps she tried to connect in a different way, to utilise a different part of herself. Maybe she just let go of trying to be connected to her inherent intuitive wisdom. I believe strongly (and our evidence collected at Sailaday OK bears this out) that when we make this connection with nature, with the nature within ourselves, we can be set free. Reducing shame can only be done within a relationship. This is a process and needs guidance and facilitation at times, as just naming your shame doesn't just happen out of the blue. There are certain requirements that need to be put in place. Here one might refer to Maslow's hierarchy of needs and, in particular, our sense of being, which for me is reinforced and enhanced when I make a connection, develop my relationship with nature and the nature within because I *am* nature. Nature is a given, it is non-judgmental and it is elemental.

This is a story of hope and what we have come to describe as 'quantum recovery'; and an example of the successes the beneficiaries of Sailaday OK could achieve.

Ten years ago, I met Alison, a beneficiary of the Sailaday OK project. She was frightened, angry and suffering the consequences of trauma. In her own words:

"I was in treatment and I was somehow persuaded much against my will to join Richard on Physis. I was terrified. My relapse on alcohol had sparked off a decline in my mental health and there followed a whole year on a psychiatric ward prior to being dumped barely functioning in the foyer of the treatment centre in Plymouth.

After two months in the residential I was offered a place on the SOK session. I was gripped by crippling anxiety and had lost any faith in my ability to function. Even on that first trip, among all the traumatic flashbacks and fits of panic something somehow 'clicked'. I had a moment at the helm when I suddenly 'got' that I was powerless over the sheer force of the elements but that I had power within that to hold and indeed influence my course. It was the closest thing to a spiritual awakening I had had in over a decade of hospital admissions due to PTSD and alcohol misuse. I believe my real recovery started that day. I have managed to hold my course. I now have my own consultancy in healthcare. Recently a colleague was observing me run a workshop with a group of doctors. He said he spotted a distinct moment when I seemed to connect, to be completely at ease with where I was and what I was doing. His words echoed almost exactly how Richard described the moment I suddenly mastered the blindfold helming. I no longer needed to be told what to do but felt it instinctively and it centred in a place other than intellect. I sensed a connection through my feet with the elements, the boat and with myself in that moment. This was the awakening I had from the Sailaday experience – this is what it gave me. A door opened and I became connected to nature and through that connection to my fragmented self. I will forever be grateful that I was persuaded to go with Sailaday those years ago. I wrote on one of the evaluation forms that four days with Sailaday had achieved what four years of other therapies have failed to achieve."

Alison is a powerful force as an NHS's Patient Champion both professionally and personally. As well as having achieved professional status, she will always support the underdog when fighting for better health care, even travelling as far as Russia and taking her place on the picket line.

Clearly something momentous happened for Alison whilst helming the boat, but until she made meaning of this experience, until she put it into words during group time and in her evaluation report and feedback, only then did she not just become more confident, but her self-esteem became more prominent. Her feelings of shame, which were being protected by her excessive fear and anxiety, became visible and she was able to step through the fear with the support of a psychotherapist offering an empathic therapeutic relationship. Consequently, the hidden monster, shame, could be brought into the light. With her increased resilience her shame became more manageable. She now had this experience of becoming a whole person – she could allow Alison to become visible. She became vulnerable and, at the risk of exposure, benefited from the results.

There are many examples in my evaluations and feedback, particularly from females who suffer a poor body image, who are crippled by the shame of what they are and their perception of how others see them. This often originates having experienced a variety of abuse as infants and young persons. Of course, this is not solely experienced by females, but our consumptive culture exacerbates these feelings of inadequacy and shame.

I hear the same sentences over and over again, maybe with slightly different combinations of words, but the meaning is just as clear when asked to perform a new task of sailing. *"Can't possibly do that", "Everyone else will be better than me", "Let someone else have a go", "I'll fail definitely, I'm so stupid and clumsy."*

It's rare, when offered the opportunity of a particular task on the boat like helming, that that person, doesn't 'have a go' eventually. With support and encouragement, they would take small steps. If they were treated as an adult with a young person's needs, to be helped and encouraged to take that first small achievable step, they normally would. I am sure that many of you will know the sensation as a parent when helping your child learn to ride a bicycle, and the first time the child realises that your hand isn't on their back supporting them physically, and they may shriek, *"Look at me, look, I can do it, I can do it."* From that moment, they're off and running or bicycling or enjoying the process of transformation.

The next step is that they cycle out of sight, then to go somewhere specific and then return home, and through all these different stages of increasing risk you are giving encouragement and praise. Likewise, on the boat, I would increase the difficulty of each task, hence the risk to their self-esteem. These increases were calibrated to fit the individual's needs and contract. Eventually they would probably take part in an exercise of Zen sailing and or blindfolded sailing, as described in earlier chapters. Both these exercises need a high degree of self-awareness and the requirement to really make that connection to the environment and the boat. To come to understand and practise using their body as an instrument for successful voyaging. They come to trust their bodies as positive instruments.

The feedback I get are many versions of the following.

"That was incredible Richard I never thought I could do that – I feel on top of the world."

"Wow, my body is fantastic – I really trust it for the first time in my life."

"I can't believe I did that! If you had told me that a week ago I would have said you were nuts."

"This feels like a whole new beginning! I'm so full of hope, seeing how my body could do all those things."

16

Batten Down the Hatches

Batten down the hatches: To prepare for inclement weather.

THANK GOD FOR supervision. I had a supervisor, David, who was experienced at working outdoors and with groups. His job was to support the supervisee, in this case me, as well as to make sure that my clients were protected, ie that the therapist he was supervising was doing a good job.

Issues cropped up several times for me, including some specific one-off difficulties. I struggled with dealing with the effect and consequences of working with these highly vulnerable and quite damaged people.

For example, at times I would work with a group from a residential centre and, perhaps 3 to 4 weeks later, I would be working with a different group from the same centre. I would be interested in how members of the previous group were progressing in their treatment and if they had left the centre, and whether it had been a good leaving or possibly a bad, premature leaving. I would sometimes be told that the person I was asking about was dead. I always found this quite shocking, because normally my last memory of them would have been them leaving the boat cheerful and optimistic, and I would have been feeling quite hopeful for their future. A common cause of death was that they had relapsed, scored from an unreliable source, and bought something that was contaminated. In almost all these cases, they had taken the same size dosage as they would have done at the height of their active addiction. Having had some weeks or months clean, their bodies just couldn't cope with the trauma and the overdose would kill them. My supervisor was good at helping me debrief.

When working with all-female or all-male groups, I was always taken by surprise that I would end up liking one group member more than the others.

Favouritism in this field would be inappropriate, so I put in a great deal of effort into disguising how I felt. My supervisor would often help me focus on the issues I had with wanting to be liked, and maybe track this back into my earlier childhood, and assist in how to set up and maintain boundaries. Even then, there were people who I ended up thoroughly disliking and I found it exhausting to maintain clear boundaries and some sort of empathic relationship with people who I honestly found very difficult.

Even though my supervisor helped me process some of these feelings, even now some of them live with me still. I remember the woman who spent a lot of the time in grief about the children she had lost to the social services due to her chaotic and abusive lifestyle. However, I would also hear her comparing notes with other members of the group, learning how to go about getting more benefits from social services if she were to have more children. This probably triggered some of the shame and grief I felt having abandoned my own children.

On another occasion, there was a man who would often, in therapy sessions, talk about his shame and sadness about the lack of love, care and money that he could offer his estranged young son. In the therapy session I could offer support and some helpful interventions about keeping boundaries and maintaining some other form of relationship with his son that didn't have to be measured by time or money. However, next morning at breakfast, I would be exasperated to hear him talking about not having any money to buy a present for his son's birthday, at the same time as discussing with the other group members the several hundreds of pounds he was about to spend on a new tattoo for himself. My feelings of exasperation and anger would nearly overwhelm me. I would find myself quite speechless and would have to find some small task I could go out and perform on the deck and get some fresh air so that I could process these feelings.

I heard some horrific stories and needed help to make sure they didn't get under my skin, as otherwise I would find them going around in my head. This was disturbing enough, but it also meant that I would find myself unable to give the participant the professional therapeutic support they needed. David, my supervisor, was great at arming me with strategies and helping me maintain my external and internal boundaries, in addition to debriefing the trauma I felt having listened to some of these tales. Occasionally, I would realise that I was being manipulated, and would have to try to work out what was the truth. However I felt about this, my job was to understand that these people were crying out for help.

I am continually staggered at how human beings can treat each other and, more specifically, how so often it seemed that young people's primary carers could be quite such abusive and horrendous human beings. I trust that I will never become unmoved by these horrific stories: the young girl who was repeatedly raped by her father; the young boy locked in a cabinet for days on end; the girl who was sold by her mother to drug dealers who were also involved in sex trading. My list became all too long, but I am proud that I could help some of these people come to terms with these traumas.

There are many first-hand accounts in this book of how people benefited from the Sailaday experience, but there were also some weird and difficult participants. This could be stressful for me, as some were just strange and hard to reach, but some so far outside my understanding that I would often feel quite powerless.

David would help me to understand countertransference in these transactions and relationships. My toxic feelings of being contaminated, stressed, powerless and overwhelmed were probably exactly what my clients were feeling. Being reminded of this, I could get my feet back on the ground by putting the content of their stories to one side and focus on dealing with the process and the core issues.

I remember working with one summer group when we had been sailing up and down the Carrick Roads river most of the day, practising and learning simple sailing skills. It was a beautiful evening, and we were sailing back up to our anchorage for the night. This stretch of country on the eastern bank is about 4 miles and comprises of a couple of creeks and little harbours and the rest is rolling countryside interspersed with woodlands and cliffs. There are farms and a series of small interlocking jigsaw-like green fields, too steep for cultivating but good for sheep and cows. Jane from London was sitting next me and on the helm. She turned to me and said, *"'ere, Richard, who mows all the fields?"* I wasn't quite sure what she was talking about to begin with, and I looked and saw where she was pointing, as there were various beautiful green fields, but I still had to think quite hard before I answered, "The cows keep the grass down". Her next remark made me want to laugh out loud: *"Why would they do that?"*

Supervision sessions had taught me to think carefully before speaking. I had learned how to do a bit more than just count to 10 before opening my mouth. At times it was hard not to show anger and irritation, or at least to temper it, so that my reply was appropriate and not too sharp. Most of the crew smoked cigarettes, on deck only, but there were many occasions, in fact most days, when my patience would be tested. We would need to undertake a sailing manoeuvre involving some or all of the crew. For example, say we were to make a tack, changing course: this had to be done efficiently and *now*, not in a few minutes' time. By this stage in the session, they would know their different tasks in this manoeuvre, and I would say... "Get ready to go about," but I would hear a shout from one of the crew: *"Hold up, I've just lit this fag, I won't be a couple of minutes."*

Some were just difficult. I can remember a man from east London, John, who really was not happy being there. There wasn't much that he enjoyed about sailing – he felt cramped in the boat, and thought it was all cold and boring. His preference was to sit down on his bunk and read a newspaper or a football magazine. It was a tiring process to keep coaxing him up to join in with the rest of the team – he was just not a team player. He was always quite open with me, willing to share what he thought about sailing and he admitted that the other people there really weren't his sort of people. One day the shout went out, "Dolphins on the port bow!" We had seen a dolphin the day before, but this was a big pod, and they were on their way over to play. I stuck my head in the cabin door and shouted down to John that there were dolphins coming up and all he could reply was, *"Okay mate, if you've seen one you've seen them all."* On the last evening of the session, participants completed evaluation forms before leaving in the morning. My habit was to defer reading these until the group had left the ship so that I had time to absorb them. I wasn't expecting much from John, but he was very gracious and grateful for the time and space I had given him. I was surprised to read that he'd learned a lot about himself. Although sailing was really not his thing, and he'd learned that he never wanted to go sailing again, he also said that listening to the others and coming to understand them, and my patience and understanding, had been a really good model for him to become a little bit more patient and had helped him to understand himself. Wow, that was unexpected!

There was a process of intake and assessment, checking on the suitability of the participants, to ensure that they had enough Adult Ego State (TA) to understand instructions. This was to ensure that they were able to get themselves as a group to Falmouth and back again, and that they were healthy and stable enough in their recovery. This was a bit of a standing joke with the care managers who were my main contacts, as there was a section that asked for details of issues they were currently dealing with. For example, craving, grief, anger, family issues, courts, money, et cetera, and suggesting they might like to add anything specific to themselves. Very often, they would glibly write *"...no, none of these, I'm fine."* The managers and I would say, "If only!", and I would make a note: "In denial."

I might ask for details about their health or medication and, if they were under a court order, I would want to know a little bit more about it. In other words, if they were meant to be doing treatment instead of going to prison.

These were people who I came to understand were not suitable sailing companions. Maybe this wasn't quite fair, but these characters were often quite disruptive. They were usually there just for a bit of a jolly, and not with the intention to effect positive changes in themselves.

There was an occasion when we had to take participants who were on court orders, and they were most definitely disruptive. I remember the last morning, I was cooking them a hot meal, as some participants had never had the experience of 'Daddy' cooking breakfast for them. We had the radio on so I could catch the weather and local news, and there was a small article about how many changes were being brought about in Cornwall due to the influx of eastern European workers. For some time, there had been a growing population of migrant workers helping with, firstly, the daffodil-picking earlier in the year, and later on picking and sorting a variety of vegetables when ready to harvest. It seemed that most Cornish people were not really prepared to do this work anymore. I made a comment about how I enjoyed the different foods that were now supplied in the big supermarkets, Romanian, Polish, and Croatian foods, and I found these people hard-working, pleasant and interesting to talk to and that they definitely brought something positive to the Cornish culture.

Three of the four participants spent a lot of their time discussing amongst themselves different ways that they could profit from the state benefit system. The two under court orders were the most vocal. They would discuss how they could maybe keep a flat they owned and not let the state benefit system know about it so they would get rehoused and then sublet one or more parts of the flat, and many other such scams. When I mentioned how helpful these immigrant workers were and how much they brought to Cornwall I was really shocked when my participants said almost with one voice, "F***ing scroungers".

This was not that uncommon a point of view but seeing as they were sitting there eating our charitably obtained provisions, were being cared for by a variety of other charities and funding, I felt sick and angry and had to leave and get some fresh air outside. After that I avoided taking people who were on court orders.

In my view, there is something wrong with a system that criminalises drug users and tries to solve a health and wellbeing issue by enforcing laws that cannot solve the real problem. The programme of decriminalisation now in place in Portugal seems highly successful and a good model that the UK could adopt. Those that are dealing and trafficking can still have the pleasure of going to prison if that's what they really desire, and maybe keep them away from those that actually need and want to change.

My relationship with our main clients, the residential centres, was deteriorating by 2016. They seemed to be under enormous financial pressures and were being asked to take on more residents for shorter periods of time and with smaller counselling teams. There also seemed to have been a growth in litigation and lawsuits from complaints, with the threat that the residents would then sue the individual counsellor or agency.

This was an extremely unfortunate development, as in this client group the resident's favourite psychological position is to be a victim, and they loved nothing more than to find somebody else to blame for their difficulties. This becomes a major stumbling block to somebody's recovery who has been encouraged to take responsibility, understand consequences, and learn acceptance.

Six weeks after the completion of a male group, we had a notice from the agencies saying that a complaint had been made against me, and that all future groups would be suspended until there was a hearing. To which we complied and requested all the information and details of the complaint.

There are quite often participants on the boat with dyslexia, and they often find it difficult when helming, particularly when I am giving them precise instructions. There is confusion, and every time they seem to have to work out which is left and which is right. Often, I have solved this problem by offering them a pair of gloves with a big 'R' on the right-hand glove and a big 'L' on the left-hand glove. One specific client was having this difficulty and I offered him the solution. He said he would think about it overnight and the next day he confirmed that it would be a really good idea and he would give it a go. His helming that day was greatly improved, and he said he found it a lot easier. There was no hint at any time that he felt shamed or abused, and his evaluation report at the end of the session was positive, with no mention of any difficulty.

What had happened in the intervening month, between the session and making the complaint, was never taken into account. Perhaps somebody else in the house had got to hear about it and was teasing him, and at that point he may well have felt shame. Nobody seemed to ask why he had taken nearly a month to make the complaint. I also had a sneaking suspicion that he enjoyed being a victim and maybe saw that there was some financial reward in it for him. I offered to have a sit down with him and offered my regrets that there had been this misunderstanding. He never replied.

Our chairman was informed that this would be referred to the Complaints Commission and we were to prepare a defence. We were informed that this was unlikely to happen until spring the following year. This would be a serious problem for the charity, and for me personally, as my governing professional body, the BACP, would also hold an enquiry. This led to a great deal of stress, depression and sleepless nights. In June the chairman of Sailaday OK was informed that no further action was to be taken. I contacted the organisation and found that this decision had been made in December, but they had not let us know. I was shocked and angry; I had found it a really distressing time, as after all those years and hundreds of people I had worked with, an official complaint had never been made. There had been misunderstandings and disagreements and some conflict on the boat, but all those things had been processed and resolved.

Shortly after this, we received a communication informing us that Longreach, the residential centre where the complaint had come from, could not afford to make any financial contributions to groups, and that they were reconsidering the usefulness of the Sailaday OK experience. Finally, we were informed that their one-day outings would be more useful to them than four days on the boat. These day trips included walks in the country, horse riding for one hour, or maybe clay pigeon shooting for the men (rather sexist). Weird and sad.

I loved working with the participants but working with that residential centre's management during the previous year had been very stressful. There had been several personnel changes in the management, people who were clearly under great stress. As a result, they had recommended for participation some highly unsuitable people.

The normal procedure would have commenced with my presentation to the residential centre earlier in the year and receive intake forms completed by staff and participants considerably in advance of the session. On this occasion, in the intake for 'J', I read that she had digestive problems. Having requested more detailed information, I received a reply from the manager to the effect that, "She was often in severe pain and had frequent hospital visits".

I could hardly believe my eyes, and thinking there must be a mistake, I emailed back, "I don't think she would be suitable for four days of marine adventure therapy". The reply came back from the residential manager: "The fresh air would do her good!" My response: "Sorry, I don't think she's a suitable candidate".

On another occasion, I was informed that the potential candidate suffered migraines. Having found no reference to suitable medication on the list provided, I contacted the referring manager for more information on the frequency of attacks and the medication prescribed for them. In reply, I was told that she had about two migraines a week lasting about 12 hours, when she needed to be in a quiet dark room having taken aspirin.

I replied to the effect that a sailing trip for four days and nights would seem highly inadvisable for her and for the rest of the group. However, I would be happy to take her if she had been prescribed an appropriate migraine medication. The response was: "I'm sure she'll be fine – the rest of the group are used to her and her migraines".

I discussed this with the Sailaday chairman and we could not believe the lack of care being shown to these very vulnerable people. A lack of care not only of the participant but also no consideration for myself and other members of the group. It would be enormously stressful to contemplate managing somebody who may need to be hospitalised, changing the dynamics of a therapeutic group.

However, later that year, I did negotiate the possibility of an occasional session with Sailaday OK. I organised a day when I would arrive at Plympton near Plymouth and give the whole residential centre an introduction to the charity – how it worked and what would happen to the participants. I had not met any of the new staff or residents since the previous year. The first difficulty was that Sailaday OK had to pay my expenses for the day as the centre had decided that they did not have the budget. Previously, they had agreed to cover this cost, as the round-trip was nearly a hundred miles. When I arrived, timed for late morning so I could have lunch with the residents, there were no staff, just a secretary and very few residents. They didn't seem to know I was coming and there were no apologies or messages. This was the final straw – working with complex and vulnerable participants was challenging but acceptable but working with careless and thoughtless clients was unacceptable.

After consulting with the chairman and the rest of the trustees, I decided not to work with this residential centre again, and it wasn't long before a similar decision was made about Closereach.

Finally, in October 2016, we arrived at the most unenviable position of having virtually no funding and very few in the way of clients. It seemed as though the Queen's Award had become the kiss of death for a failing charity.

17

Toe the Line

Toe the line or *Toe the mark:* At parade, sailors and soldiers were
required to stand in line, their toes in line with a seam of the deck.

AT THE BEGINNING of each day on the boat, before breakfast and as soon as
everyone was awake and conscious, we would have a short session of what I
called meditation, but these days would probably be called "mindfulness".
This was a process of tuning into the here and now, to have some time
dedicated to stillness. Time to find oneself, and to make some space for the
coming day.

In good weather, we would sit in the cockpit, in the open air. If it was
too cold or wet, we would meet together down below in the main cabin. On
the first morning, I would brief them about the purpose of the exercise, ask
them to sit comfortably and for 5 or 10 minutes make sure they were warm.
I would make it clear that it was not a competition, something they had to
try hard to get right, but a time to just surrender to the moment, be present
and follow instructions.

The first stage, lasting about 5 minutes, was to relax mind and body by
using their breathing. Focusing on the face, close the eyes and take a big
breath in through the nose and out through the open mouth, letting go of
all tension around the eyes, mouth and jaw, and blowing any tightness out
through the mouth. Then, to release any tensions in the body, starting from
the head, then the neck, shoulders, and so on down, I would ask them to
take a breath in and, with the mind's eye, focus on each part in turn. Then,
breathing out slowly, let go of any tension. I would talk them through this
with a gentle monotonous tone to encourage them to relax and be at ease.

The next part of the process, if we were outside, would be to turn their attention to all the sounds around them. I found that most of them needed some sort of focus, as it was too much to ask them to just stay with the emptiness and peace. I would suggest that they accept the sounds around them for exactly what they were – a series of different noises. The birdsong was not birdsong, but just a different sound from the wind in the rigging. They should not try to make any sense or meaning of the sounds, but to 'get out of their heads', just surrender, and accept the sensation of sound. All very Zen!

If the weather made it impossible to be outdoors, then we would be down in the cabin, and the brief there was to just focus on the sensations of the movement of the body as you sat glued to your seat. The boat would be responding to wind and waves and, to maintain a sitting position, you would be flexing ever so slightly to maintain a sitting posture. Usually very subtle movements, small sensations of change as you flex.

I would encourage people to use their breathing to help them come back to the point of focus when they realised that they had wandered off in their heads, and this might happen quite often. As I had explained, this was not a competition, but a process of allowing space and time to get away from all the clutter, all the dirty washing flapping around inside their heads. To find some relief, possibly even a little bit of peace.

After about five minutes, I would ask them to deepen their breathing, and to notice the changes in the body from taking those bigger breaths. Feel the air in through the nostrils and out through the mouth, sensations of an expanding chest and lungs, and to notice the thoughts that might creep in at that moment. I would then talk them through what I consider is a process of grounding, a process I suggested that could be used at any time, at any moment of stress, anxiety, fear or feeling of being overwhelmed and powerless.

While their eyes were closed, I would ask them to put their hands together and notice the feeling, or maybe touch the cloth of their trousers – texture and temperature. Then notice what they could smell, lick their lips and notice what they might taste. With eyes still closed I would ask them to notice what they could hear. This was connecting them with a basic reality, as these four senses were all they had at that moment in time. The next step would for them was to try to make sense of these feelings, but I would explain that they needed to trust their senses, accept reality and know that something feels rough or smooth, wet or cold.

I appreciated that some would find difficulty with the meditation session, or perhaps would like a quick method of grounding at any time. I would suggest that they might have a Polo mint, a hot drink or, for smokers, a cigarette. To take the mint in their hands and feel it, notice one side is smooth and one-side rough, notice it is round with a hole in the middle, to notice its smell, taste and texture and only then to put it in their mouth and notice the changes that happened. Whatever the chosen activity, to take time over it, enjoy immersing oneself in this little adventure. A great way to get some relief from craving, from mental and emotional distress. Not a cure-all, but a little moment of peace, some relief and reassurance.

In my own early stages of recovery I was taught a similar process, as I found that in group therapy the urge to run was so strong. The scream in my body made me ache to get out of there, and I would feel so overwhelmed with emotion, grief, anxiety bordering on terror that I found it almost impossible to take part in these groups and stay for one hour. My counsellor taught me this simple technique: to just touch your nose or somewhere not noticeable to everybody else and just take a moment to register the temperature, texture and any other sensations that were connected to that touch. Look up at the ceiling and check that the roof hadn't fallen in, that you were still there, and that you were okay. That was when I began to be able to take part in the therapy. I might have had to do this repeatedly several times during the group in the early days.

Most participants benefited from these moments at the beginning of each day. It gave them a chance to leave behind whatever might have been going on during the night, when one can get lost in nightmares, monsters, fears and doubts – the darkness that can steal your serenity. They mostly enjoyed the rediscovery of what a simple world might sound and feel like, before their cluttered minds would take over and distort the truth. Most of them could rarely stay focused for more than 10 or 20 seconds in any of the exercises before their minds wandered off into the past or the future, but most would take a breath, spend some energy exhaling and letting go of those thoughts and come back to what they could hear or feel.

However, some found it extremely difficult, stressful and painful to sit there and do virtually nothing. They couldn't follow what I was saying, perhaps because their bodies were in panic mode and ready to run or fight. In the early days of teaching these techniques, I wondered if I was doing something wrong, or they weren't focusing well enough or maybe just being belligerent. The idea that somebody couldn't just quietly sit there listening to the call of the seagull, the lapping of the water on the hull, or the wind in the rigging was difficult to understand. I asked for help from my supervisor and from my wife Sue, a skilled practising psychotherapist.

It was important for me to understand that, for very vulnerable and damaged people, there is a shadow side to these exercises. I was aware that I was asking everyone to be mindful of every exercise we did on the boat. However, as I read more, I came to a deeper understanding of some of the pitfalls and dangers in using mindfulness. Sue was very helpful; I can quote here from some of her research.

"Mindfulness-based therapy in the South London and Maudsley NHS foundation trust has researched this area for **ten** years and says, 'Certain mental health problems increase the risk of adverse effects of mindfulness'; he particularly mentions PTSD and bipolar conditions 'which many don't know they have until they surface through particular life events including attempting mindfulness practice'."[1] SPH 2019

Speaking about mindfulness interventions in education[2] Knightsmith (cited Bloom, 2017), vice-chair of the Children and Young People's Mental Health Coalition, said such exercises could be "actively harmful for those who are particularly vulnerable or have a history of trauma" and "if a child is suffering abuse at home, being given space and time for thoughts to drift through your head isn't necessarily good... schools need to be aware of the potential risks, even with the most seemingly nice of interventions."

A further ethical issue is that mindfulness is being used in military populations to manage high stress situations. It is being taught to soldiers to support them to remain focused in extreme stress environments, to quickly absorb large amounts of information and make effective decisions without becoming overwhelmed. One form is Mindfulness-Based Mind Fitness Training, a 20-hour course designed to increase resilience to stress. Titmuss believes that "military mindfulness and psychology will provide soldiers and drone pilots with *mental armour* so they can base their decisions on what is in front of them."

Transforming life's archaic experiences (trauma) and current experiences and creating and maintaining intimacy in relationships depends on the ability to differentiate and express the discrete processing emotions. This in turn depends on the ability to put left-brain language to right-brain experience

---

1   Additionally, Florian Ruths' 'Clinical lead for mindfulness-based therapy in the South London and Maudsley National Health Service foundation trust,' who has "researched this area for 10 years," has noted that "certain mental health problems increase the risk of adverse effects of mindfulness." (Ruths, cited in Foster, 2016, para. 24). In terms of such increased risk, Ruths mentions PTSD and bipolar conditions in particular, how "many people may not know they have a bipolar vulnerability until they try mindfulness. Or they might have repressed the symptoms of post-traumatic stress disorder, only for these to emerge after trying the practice." (Ruths, cited in Foster, 2016, para. 27)

2   Dr P Knightsmith, pooky@inyourhands.com

(physical sensations). Language development is a social process; the capacity for emotional processing cannot be developed alone.

Kornfield (2012),[3] a psychologist with 40 years of mindfulness teaching and practice experience says of mindfulness, "While wonderful, it often left untouched childhood wounds, unconscious fears, loneliness, poor self-care, troubles at work, and difficulties handling feelings and intimate relationships.

From my relational psychotherapist perspective, one of the reasons that mindfulness doesn't do it all is because of the lack of attention to naming experience."

I think it's important for psychotherapists to be clearer about the strengths, limitations and potential negative side effects of mindfulness and how mindfulness and psychotherapy can complement each other in alleviating seemingly ever-increasing levels of human suffering.

I came to understand why meditation or mindfulness exercises were not a cure-all and my reason for maintaining the practice was solely to give participants a different experience of reality; a quick and easy-to-use tool to help them exist in the present. I was also aware that, as with any of the other exercises on the boat, they had to be complemented by giving time to name the experience when in relationship to others. I would strive to maintain a balance between *Being, Doing* and *Thinking*.

Whether it is partaking in some activity such as sailing a boat or sitting quietly and contemplating the world of sound, I would be entering a state of well-being, trusting my physical sensations as truth – an unarguable foundation for reality.

Most of the participants arrived with a willingness to partake in this experience, to make some positive changes in their behaviour and attitudes, to take stock of who they are now and to celebrate the changes they had already made. However, many of them brought with them – quite unconsciously, until it was pointed out to them – a dead weight, an escape route, a means of flight, a way to connect with an unnatural world.

I could not ban mobile phones but with each group I agreed boundaries around the use of them. I would advise participants to tell those back at home and ashore that they might not hear from them for four days unless there is an emergency. I usually made the same tired old joke that there might also be quite a lot of people who might not even notice that they had gone away, and that the world will continue with or without them. I asked them to keep their phones switched off between breakfast and dinner in the evening, and

---

3   Jack Kornfield 2011 *Lamp in the Darkness* ISBN 978-1-60407-642-4

I asked them also to be aware of what happens internally when they might see on their phone that a call has come through or that a text is waiting to be read. Be aware of the tug, be aware of the hold this object has over you. Right now, today, it is not helping you.

The mentoring groups, my RATs, usually came to understand the benefits of leaving their phones at home, that they are actually an impediment if you are trying to connect with nature without and nature within.

Personally, my phone is important to me while away on the boat. It is a good means of communication for safety and for friends and family. It is also an amazing source of information for weather, tides, navigation and news. I have noticed that when I'm on the boat for some days and nights, I have a much better internal knowledge of time. If I wake up during the night, which I often will, maybe several times, I do not have to look at my watch and yet I will know the time within five or 10 minutes. When I'm ashore, after a few nights this skill disappears.

So, the poor old mobile phone has become a symbol of our divorce from our natural state. Some participants would tell me they had 250 friends but felt unloved. They had endless information at hand, but little knowledge of the world or how to be in it. They could spend their nights gambling or watching pornography as long as there was a signal.

Theodore Roszak (1995)[4] has claimed that contemporary technological and industrial society has severed people's deep connection to nature, and I agree with this, feeling that we need to strive to repair this relationship. When I work with people in repairing this relationship there is a reconciliation and recovery. Shepherd suggests that people as a society are acting abnormally because they cannot reconcile this internal struggle. What once was a self-identity derived from a deep profound relationship to the natural world is now shaped by a highly industrialised technological society that we often feel powerless to control.

The purchasing of consumer of goods fills an 'empty self' "...by giving us immediate pleasure and achievement while at the same time possibly conferring status and recognition". Psychologist Philip Cushman (1990) described the empty self as seeking the experience of being continually filled by consumer goods, experiences, calories and romantic partners to combat our growing alienation and fragmentation.

Society is forever erecting barriers between its citizens and the inner/ outer wilderness. On the outer side, we have our air-conditioned houses and

---

4   Theodore Roszak first came to public prominence in 1969 with the publication of his *The Making of the Counterculture*, the first use of the term counterculture and ecopsychologists; and 1995 *Restoring the Earth*.

cars, gated communities and indoor malls, fences and animal control officers, dams and virtual realities. On the inner side, we are offered prescribed 'mood enhancers', alcohol, and street drugs; consumerism and dozens of other soul-numbing addictions; fundamentalisms, transcendentalisms, and other escapisms; rigid belief systems as to what is "good" and what is "bad"; and teachings that God or some other paternal figure will watch over us and protect our delicate lives.

For me, this feels so close to a description of addiction in one form or another that we seem to be suffering from as a culture. This addiction characterises every aspect of industrial society: dependence on alcohol, food, drugs, as much as a dependence on career achievement, prestige, wealth, more ingenious weaponry and the need to exercise control over everything.

There is a trauma of abandonment and separation from nature, our perceived powerlessness at being stuck in this industrialised technological information-driven society dependent on consumption and consumerism. It is argued by some that it has created a civilisation that is dysfunctional, possibly autistic, and that we exhibit many of the symptoms of PTSD. One of the behavioural symptoms of trauma is addictive behaviour.

We seem to suffer from the shame of having 'fallen from grace'[5] which perpetuates this rupture, this separation, and I recognise this in my deep yearning to connect with nature.

---

5 'fallen from grace' which perpetuates this rupture, this separation; also see fallen angel; in theology is about humanity's original innocence and happiness resulting from adding the needs eating the fruit in the garden of Eden, also see 'original sin.'

18

Taken Aback

Taken aback: Inattentive helmsmen might allow the dangerous situation to arise where the wind is blowing into the sails 'backwards', causing a sudden (and possibly dangerous) shift in the position of the sails.

AT THE BEGINNING of 2016 I was feeling excited and hopeful, having received confirmation of my award of the British Empire Medal in the Queen's Honours List. It had generated quite a lot of interest locally; I was invited for interview with the local press and radio stations, and the maritime community were really interested to hear why I had been given this Award. This generally filled me with hope and optimism for the coming year.

Sadly, my optimism was short-lived. This was also the occasion when I received notification of the formal complaint made by one of the participants against me personally, referred to in an earlier chapter, and which left me full of dread and distress.

The first action of Longreach, the organisation making the complaint, was to terminate any contract with Sailaday OK in 2016 until the issue was resolved. Sailaday's chairman, Bill Jerrom, was extremely supportive and did everything he could to back me up through this difficult time. We also offered to sit down with the complainant, to apologise for any hurt that might have been felt. However, we were informed that it would be referred to the local safeguarding panel/board and to the Care Quality Commission. The complaint would then become official, with possible ramifications for me as a professional psychotherapist and certainly for Sailaday OK's activities.

So, already we were starting with one significant client less at the beginning of the year, the time when we usually reviewed contracts with our main clients. At the same time, our other major client, Closereach, informed us that their funding had been reduced considerably and would only be available for outdoor sessions for the men's residential centre. The only funding for women was for indoor sessions such as homebuilding, parenting, yoga, knitting and domestic skills. Incredible. I found it hard to believe, firstly that only men would benefit from outdoor experiences, and secondly that they thought of Sailaday OK as just an outdoor activity. They seemed to have completely lost sight of its therapeutic value. A new contract was negotiated with Longreach, but with limited bookings based on Sailaday bearing the cost of providing and provisioning the sessions, if they agreed to cover the cost of getting their clients to and from Falmouth.

Our next bad news was that Addaction had also decided they couldn't afford the £10 per person that we asked them for, to help cover our expenses for a one-day session for young people. This seemed petty compared to the several hundred pounds they spent on taxis ferrying people to and from their homes, which could be anywhere from Bude to Penzance, to Falmouth and back.

Suddenly, the future looked bleak. I was feeling stressed, anxious and upset about the complaint that had been made against me. I had worked with up to 60 people each year through the 10 years without one official complaint. There had always been room on the boat to discuss or voice any negative stuff that might have cropped up and it was usually dealt with there and then. When working with this client group,[1] negative transference and negative projections onto the therapist are normal. When they occur in therapy, I always consider it an opportunity to work with the issue at hand. To try and clear some of the old beliefs that this figure of authority is there to hurt them, harm them, abuse them. I am not their father, teacher, or other figure of authority.

Vulnerable and traumatised people such as those we worked with are quite likely to, and do usually, take the psychological position of the victim. In their experience, it has been useful for them to have others to blame for their situation. "It's Dad's fault", "It's a policeman's fault", or "It's my wife's fault". "It's because they did this or that to me". The hardest part of early recovery is for them to take responsibility, take ownership of, not just the events that happened to them but also of their feelings. So, it really was quite remarkable that there had been no official complaints. I probably had worked with hundreds of women, many of whom would have loved to find a man to blame

---

1 Negative transference and negative projections: when working with this specific client group, negative transference and negative projections are very helpful insights into the clients' psychological make-up.

for their circumstances and to project on to them all that negativity, but this had never happened. There has been disagreement and conflict, anger and tears, but there has also been created massive positive changes in attitudes and beliefs about themselves and the world around them.

So, after all these years of great feedback, evaluations and proof of positive changes, it felt like it was all being thrown back at me. The voice in my head was saying, "How could they believe that bastard? What on earth made them think, after all my history with them, that I would behave like that, and that therefore they could accept his word over mine?" The anger was building up in my head; not a very therapeutic reaction, to the point where I really didn't think I could work with them again. Their general attitude seemed to have shifted enormously, probably due to multiple changes in staff and management; it appeared to me that they failed to see any therapeutic value in having such an intense marine residential therapeutic experience.

Thinking that things couldn't really get any worse and, buoyed up by the award ceremony and our visit to London, I was really shocked when we had our latest Big Lottery application turned down. We had contacts within the organisation and had several supportive and helpful phone and email communications with them. However, we were then referred to a new area manager for the south west of England for Big Lottery funding applications. She was extremely negative and more or less said that we hadn't a "hope in hell" of achieving the sort of funding we were applying for. Her argument seemed to be based on her misunderstanding of what and who we were, and she insisted that there were too many other people like us doing the same thing. Unbelievable! If they couldn't see how unique and trail-blazing we were and understand the life-changing experiences that our participants went through, then I really began to feel that I could not carry on fighting the good fight any longer.

Normally, by June we would have been in a flurry of sessions, two or more a month, and one-day sessions with young people. Not this year. My relationships with the women's residential centre, Longreach, were getting more and more fraught, as evidenced by the difficulties I had been having with inappropriate referrals.

Again, after consulting with the Chair and the trustees, I decided to stop working with Longreach residential centre, and it wasn't long until a similar decision was made about Closereach. In June, nearly 6 months after being told that the complaint would be passed on officially, probably involving my attendance at the hearing, I received that letter referred to in any earlier chapter to the effect that no more action would be taken. I was so angry and frustrated to discover that that decision had been made in February, but they hadn't bothered to tell me or the trustees.

I ran one group that year from Closereach, which was shambolic in its organisation: management intakes were not completed, participants who said they were going to arrive didn't, and replacements were sent without any word to me.

It was all too much – I had had enough. My stress levels were going through the roof and I felt permanently angry and depressed. I must have been hell to live with. There was something familiar about the sensation of being on a battlefield, fighting to survive, rolling an enormous boulder up the hill, only to be flattened when it rolled down just when we reached the top, and having to start all over again.

This was not the only area of my life that seemed to be falling apart, disintegrating and going down the chute. I could see no rays of sunshine in the future. At the end of June 2016, I hosted an exhibition of paintings in St Ives with my good friend Colin; we shared a venue and expenses. We both thought this would be excellent timing as it was just before 'bucket and spade holidays' started in July and it was a well-known gallery right in the centre of St Ives. The previous year I had held two other solo exhibitions but had sold no paintings. In St Ives I sold one to a family member. Part of me understood that the recession and economic changes that the UK was going through might be to blame, but also there was another voice in my head being highly critical of my artistic ability. In fact, I really had forgotten why on earth I was doing this.

Enough was very nearly enough. I remember in my days of drinking and drug-taking when I was often asked whether I'd had enough. I seemed to have gone round in circles again; I was negotiating with myself, reality versus denial. I was waking up most mornings feeling depressed and waiting for the sword of Damocles to finally fall on me, feeling fragmented and angry. I had this existential sensation of having to fight to survive. The idea of letting go of the charity filled me with grief and despair, and a wicked voice in my head kept telling me I'd f*****d up.

19

No Room to Swing a Cat

No room to swing a cat: The entire ship's company
was expected to witness floggings, assembled on deck.
If it was very crowded, the bosun might not have
room to swing the 'cat o' nine tails' (the whip).

WHEN CONSIDERING IDEAS for a more ambitious application for Big Lottery funding, I paid quite a lot of attention to finding a way for the charity to be more self-supporting in the future; for example, owning a much larger vessel which could work for its living all year round. After a lot of complicated discussion and paperwork, we launched our self-sufficiency drive by opening a trading company and a limited company to support the charity.

This went hand in hand with my rethinking around the ethos and purpose of adventure therapy. I believe this started in Denver when talking to other therapists who were working with nature. Not just looking at what they were doing and how they integrated the therapy with nature, but also acquiring quite a long reading list of their books, which were more about the development of soul and our relationship to nature.

Dissatisfaction with the process of adventure therapy had been growing in me for some time. Historically and globally, since the industrial revolution, and certainly in the development of the military/industrial complex, humanity has tended to go out and use nature for its own benefit and not put a great deal back. I had been feeling the same way about adventure therapy as, since its early days of the Woodsmen of central Europe, the Scouts and even Hitler Youth, or Duke of Edinburgh Award, we have been encouraged to behave in the same manner. To go out into nature, take what is useful for us without giving anything back. I was beginning to lean towards eco-therapy rather than using nature to have an adventure based on self-interest. In eco-therapy we can regain some balance and learn from nature – nature will deliver what we need if we listen.

Adventure/eco-therapy is not new: "It's our condition that has changed." (RH)

The use of the wilderness as a part of the healing process and traditional rites of passage into adulthood can be traced back in history to many cultures; we were doing this thousands of years ago. A process of immersion into the wilderness was prevalent in Celtic and Druid Britain, Native Americas, Africa, and in Jewish and Christian traditions, and most tribal cultures. Celtic evidence of rites of passage is all around us, particularly here in Cornwall.

What once was a self-identity derived from a deep and profound relationship to the natural world is now shaped by a highly industrialized technological society driven by consumption. As Paul Wachtel (1989, p. 71) wrote, "The idea of more, of ever-increasing wealth, has become the centre of our identity, and our security, and we are caught by it as the addict is caught by his drugs." I can identify with the proponents of eco-psychology who believe that we struggle as individuals to define ourselves in a technological and consumer-driven world. We hear many voices begging us to change our consumption habits and the way we live and there are many examples of the social, economic and environmental effects of our dysfunctional behaviour. Yet, we cannot resist buying a bottle of water, a sport utility vehicle, the latest smartphone, or a laptop computer to satisfy our perceived needs. As an addict struggles to control his or her desire to consume a drug, humans struggle to control their desires to consume products that make them feel better. Purchasing consumer goods fills an 'empty self' by producing immediate pleasure and achievement, while often conferring status and recognition. I have certainly come to understand from my own personal experience that there is a lost or forgotten aspect of my self-identity that strives to reconnect with nature. The more isolated humans become from the natural world, the more difficult it becomes for them to grasp or understand the struggle in which they are engaged. This causes anxiety, which results in abnormal or irrational behaviour and a desire to reconcile internal conflict. What once was a self-identity derived from a deep and profound relationship to the natural world is now shaped by a highly industrialised technological society driven by consumption.

The programme I was devising for use on the boat was, on the surface, similar to what I had been doing, but I was redefining the theory behind it. I had simply started to understand from reading and from my own experience that 'I am nature'. It is not something external, to be exploited or enjoyed for a moment and then retreated from. I am part of the corruption, the underlying sense of loss.

"Experiencing a spiritual encounter with nature means one can touch upon deep parts of one's personality, receive profound insights, and sense a strong connection to the universe. A direct encounter with natural elements can trigger strong emotions and sensations". RH 2012

Let us now look again at *St. George and the Dragon*. In a later version of the legend, St. George travelled for many months by land and sea until he came to Libya.

Here he met a poor hermit who told him that everyone in that land was in great distress, for a dragon had long ravaged the country.

'Every day,' said the old man, 'he demands the sacrifice of a beautiful maiden and now all the young girls have been killed. The king's daughter alone remains, and unless we can find a knight who can slay the dragon she will be sacrificed tomorrow. The king of Egypt will give his daughter in marriage to the champion who overcomes this terrible monster.'

When St. George heard this story, he was determined to try and save the princess, so he rested that night in the hermit's hut, and at daybreak set out to the valley where the dragon lived. When he drew near, he saw a little procession of women, headed by a beautiful girl dressed in pure Arabian silk. The princess Sabra was being led by her attendants to the place of death. The knight spurred his horse and overtook the ladies. He comforted them with brave words and persuaded the princess to return to the palace. Then he entered the valley.

As soon as the dragon saw him it rushed from its cave, roaring with a sound louder than thunder. Its head was immense and its tail fifty feet long. But St. George was not afraid. He struck the monster with his spear, hoping he would wound it.

The dragon's scales were so hard that the spear broke into a thousand pieces. And St. George fell from his horse. Fortunately, he rolled under an enchanted orange tree against which poison could not prevail, so that the venomous dragon was unable to hurt him. Within a few minutes he had recovered his strength and was able to fight again.

He smote the beast with his sword, but the dragon poured poison on him and his armour split in two. Once more he refreshed himself from the orange tree and then, with his sword in his hand, he rushed at the dragon and pierced it under the wing where there were no scales, so that it fell dead at his feet.

What I find interesting about this particular version of the St George and the Dragon story is the power invested in the orange tree, the symbol for healing, growth and change. Nature overcoming all poisons eventually.

This differs from the *St George and the Dragon* that I knew was a young child and which had been my favourite bedtime reading from Dad. That was a theatre played out in my earlier life, as this early version of St George mirrored my addictions, chasing dragons and going from one dragon to the next, along with his preference for rescuing ladies. It was all a very co-dependent process and again you are going from one site to another to rescue yet again another lady. Side note to this is that a method of taking heroin is called chasing the dragon, where you smoke it through a tube from a piece of foil with flame underneath it.

I devised a programme of marine eco-therapy, offering free one- or two-day taster sessions to some of the eco-psychology proponents I had met. The feedback was extremely positive and helped me to improve and develop some of the exercises. Unfortunately, the cost of running four-day sessions was quite prohibitive and nobody felt able to come up with the money for this experience. Looking back, maybe it was just as well that I didn't use my time rather arrogantly leading other people down a path into a wilderness that I hadn't yet fully comprehended and understood myself.

There was another circle which had started in 1968, and which was now reaching completion. I had become dissatisfied with the liberal Marxist student politics of that time. In Paris 1968, the poster I was familiar with said: *"Be realistic, demand the Impossible"*, and another, more Marxist thought: *"It is forbidden to forbid"*. In 1968 the student protests descended into a general paralysis of Parisian life as the students were joined by the workers. For a brief moment, something like the re-enactment of the 1871 Paris commune had seemed possible.

That year is significant for a number of reasons. Firstly, the student protesters represented the first real upsurge of unofficial politics in post-war Western Europe. We were hardly Marxist in the orthodox sense of the term but what became more accurately known as 'situationists'. New liberal economics triumphed over the political but this created a space for the globalisation of an economic system with no accountability. Global corporations and the post-modern state of economics, directly accountable to no-one but themselves and the shareholders, resulting in an economic domain even more detached from political control. Within this I felt lost and powerless. My only source of spiritual food and guidance is my connection to, and trust in, nature.

This other interpretation of *St George and the Dragon* differs from the one at the start of this book, that one I interpreted on a more personal level about addictions and my psychological makeup. This more recent version or at least more recent to this book may have other interpretations. To see the king maybe as the state, the maidens and daughter as the victims, the dragon the symbol of the global industrial military capitalist liberalisation, and its gold stored coveted and hoarded at the expense of the planet but when exhausted we will all eventually pay for it. And George, who is he, the hero, rescuer, and ultimately a saint, a man who possibly achieves spiritual enlightenment.

I was coming to comprehend that my connection to nature was pivotal in maintaining my sanity in a world in which I had very little impact and could only watch the insanity around me. This was taking me to a new level of acceptance and surrender, the opposite of fighting and trying. A more spiritual approach was required.

I needed help in this process but found that, for me, traditional psychotherapy was not effective in these circumstances. I was recommended to contact a shaman, David, who ran *Northern Drum*, offering shamanic workshops, courses and vision quests. As far as I could tell, my sessions with David were exactly what I had been looking for. He helped me define some actions that needed to be taken and to recognise the strength of my relationship with nature, particularly the element of water. We also came to understand there was an imbalance of earth and fire, resulting in my commitment to spend time during the autumn and winter on my own in an earthbound environment.

Taking my pasty for lunch, I would sit in Tehidy Woods and immerse myself in the sounds of the rocks and crows or running water. I would watch the birds and squirrels, be aware of sunlight and rain, and the changes in light and colours. To be solitary – no book, no smartphone, just me, the pasty and my immediate environment. I made plans to go away that winter to a completely different place, but chose Morocco, where I had friends. I felt confident enough to travel south on my own by car and sleep rough in the environment bordering the desert. I prepared myself for the coming year, of letting go of Sailaday OK, ridding myself of debt, and making space for change within myself.

I had the sense of walking into brick walls – whichever way I looked or attempted to journey I was thwarted. I seemed to have drifted or been blown into a new stage in my living. I realised I was entering my mid-60s. Physically, mentally, emotionally, and in particular, spiritually, my needs were changing, and I had to adapt and prepare to take on the role of a more elderly member of the community. Maybe that was what the sense of having to fight to survive was telling me – it was time to let go, move on, and accept the unknown.

David's support and understanding gave me the strength to make another huge change in my life and come to terms with what I considered my final addiction. My addiction to debt. It seems strange, writing this now, how I can clearly see a linear process between complete trust and belief in nature to heal, not just my wounds, but those of the entire world, had led me into my last (I hope) addiction – that of accumulating financial debt. It seems to be the overriding global capitalistic process of annihilating this planet, and I have been a full-time player.

Most of my working life, I have been able to find ways and means of making money – not really accumulating it but making just enough. I was opportunistic and able to take advantage of my circumstances. Sometimes it was by hard work, often quite creatively; I always had the ability to find something that was saleable to make cash. Sometimes legal, sometimes not so legal. Underlying the whole process was a belief that if and when I didn't have enough, I could borrow, and use that money to make money. It seemed like a really good idea at the time – if I were short of money, I could borrow it, and it didn't worry me if I was borrowing more than I was making. For most of the 80s and 90s it was easy to borrow from banks, in fact they were usually falling over themselves to lend money, and it was easy to fake figures for mortgages, life insurance etc.

Thinking now about that process, I can link it very clearly to my addiction to chemicals. If I had emotional problems, or issues with relationships or work, taking lots of drugs and alcohol usually sorted it out. In fact, drugs and alcohol solved most of my problems. Life was much better when I took lots of chemicals. Until it wasn't.

For 10 years my income had been seasonal, so income from sailing was above and beyond my daily needs for six months of the year. However, income from painting was lowest during the winter, so I relied more and more on credit, switching cards to make sure that I maintained zero interest rates. During the summer and higher earning periods I would attempt to pay off some of my credit cards. This sort of worked for a while, but my pile of credit cards increased over the years, together with the extent of my debt, which became untenable during times when earnings from sailing and painting were at a low ebb. "Untenable" doesn't really sum up the feelings attached to that debt, feelings of hopelessness, despair and powerlessness. I was paying, just in interest, about £2,000 a month at the last count. Just as was the case with my chemical addictions, I was using credit cards to survive and even to help pay off other credit cards. Madness. In fact, it was unbelievable that I hadn't recognised this madness and the insanity of my behaviour, partly because I was ashamed and couldn't tell anybody. When I started to talk about it, I was struck by the madness, and the shame and denial that was keeping it all in place.

The Moroccan trip planned for the end of the year, probably over Christmas, was an opportunity to prepare myself for this major letting go, this acceptance and preparing myself to be guided out of this dark place. As when I had been forced to accept that I couldn't handle my chemical addictions on my own, I needed help. I found practical help from the charity, One Step. I also needed to renew my relationship with God, who I could find within myself when I was calm, clear and fully integrated into my internal and external nature.

There was a step that needed to be taken first and I must thank David for helping me to recognise the importance of the process of saying "goodbye" and "thank you". Through meditation together and counselling we defined a quest that needed to be undertaken.

Shamanic quest or, in this case, vision quest was to give me a time of solitude in nature, where profound spiritual guidance and healing could be found. This guidance and healing could relate to a specific area of my life. A period of at least three days alone in nature was required, of fasting, praying, meditation, and allowing my mind to move into a place of stillness. Hopefully, I could distinguish my true self from some the chatter in my head and allow space for the mystery of the future to come into my life and show me a way forward. A quest might help reveal to me my life's purpose and at least my appreciation and gratitude for life. To help me consciously make a choice about moving forward into a new life phase.

These were some of the goals that David helped me define, and the process was fairly simple. The maritime element of water was the environment I was happiest in, and I was fully prepared to immerse myself in that form of nature, probably through three or four days on the boat. Most vision quests are solitary events with possibly a guide to help interpret the outcomes. The most familiar would be spending time underground or in dark places, and maybe the use of fire and the event of dawn as the culmination of the process.

I clearly wanted to pay homage and express gratitude for all that the natural environment had given me. To give thanks by focusing my mind and body, possibly culminating in making an offering. Keeping in mind some of the ancient gods that ruled this watery world. The Roman god of the sea, Neptune, was first to come to mind, then the Greek Poseidon and Aphrodite, and, of course, not forgetting Thor, the Viking god of the weather. There were too many Indian gods to keep in mind – an almost endless list!

I know that when I lose contact with the sense of gratitude for all that I have, I am likely to struggle. I have lived a very full life and survived many life-threatening situations. Some have said that it's miraculous that I have a life at all today. However, I don't see it as miraculous – I see it as a logical result of a process, that when followed and adhered to, life becomes full and meaningful.

When I become disconnected, feeling loveless when around Sue my soul partner, we move into conflict and fragmentation. An effort needs to be made to move toward, and this includes acceptance, and surrender but not in a passive form, in a form of dynamic energy. The goal is love.

20

Cut and Run

Cut and run: When wanting to make a quick escape, a ship's crew might cut lashings to sails or cut anchor cables, causing damage to the rigging, or losing an anchor, but shortening the time needed to make ready by bypassing the proper procedures.

IN THE LATE autumn of 2016, I undertook my vision quest – four days of solitude on *Physis*. It was not intended to be a period of high activity involving sailing or testing myself against the marine environment, but simply a calm period of contemplation, meditation and reflection on my situation and the environment. I decided to take a minimum of things that could distract me; I took my phone, but only for safety reasons. I chose reading material that would help me deepen my understanding of where I was and vowed not to refer to the radio and other outside influences such as the news and social media.

For some time, I had been thinking about what my offering might be. What could I offer that was symbolic and had some profound meaning for me. My list was long, but it became shorter when I explored the criteria for the gift. Not too valuable, possibly something I could let sink in the sea but would not cause discomfort or heartache to someone if it was given away. My mind was going through a hundred different things and I realised I couldn't think it through – I had to step back and let it come to me. The next afternoon I had been sitting at home looking out into the garden pondering on this quest offering when my eyes locked on to a cast brass sculpture of my head that my mother had sculpted when I was about 20 or 21. I had never felt a great attachment to it, and yet there must have been one as it had followed me around all my adult life. Here it still was 45 years later, sitting amongst the plants, being decorative in a garden in Cornwall. Perfect, this was definitely something of me, something of my past, something of my connection to my birth and life, and something heavy.

The autumn weather was unpredictable as I moved out of my safe mooring at Port Navas[1] and anchored in a small, secluded bay near the mouth of the Helford estuary. This bay with its little beach, cliffs and dense foliage held memories of ancient times in another life with my children when they were young, when we had escaped down here from work and drugs. The weather was getting a bit wild coming up from the south west, and we were sheltered in our bay as a white-water charged past only yards away. We were in a little pool of tranquility, even though the wind howled in the trees above us.

The first day, I just acclimatised myself to this new regime, including having to deal with the obvious boredom. It was very easy, or it would have been very easy, to go out and charge about in that very attractive sailing environment: quite strong winds, moderate seas, white water, plenty of excitement and adrenaline to be experienced out there. Some time was spent experiencing and feeling this drive to be busy, doing, active, accepting that this was my way. Not searching for the other part of me that needed to be still even though the world around me was highly active and at times quite threatening.

By the afternoon of day two, I had rationalised that I did actually need to experience this other connection to the environment. To sail in it, react to it, allow myself to be part of it, to be at the mercy of it, and yet to find a way of moving forward towards a destination. So, I decided to sail to the Dodman headland or, as it used to be called, The Deadman. This was a fairly strenuous sail, with a south-westerly wind allowing me to sail a broad reach there and back. The waves were breaking over the deck, the wind was gusting force five or six and it was exhilarating. After some time at the helm, I realised I was humming some sort of tune or noise in sympathy with the whistling and howling of the wind in the rigging. I became more and more conscious of this noise up above me or around me, the waves sounding like trains charging past as they coursed under me. The noise of the rigging was awesome, musical and frightening at the same time. I began to tune into this sound, this very elemental rhythmical voice or voices. I began to imitate it; I gave way to it and really filled my lungs and sang/shouted louder and louder. Until the rigging and I were howling at each other like wolves howling at the moon – we worked together, creating a new sound. Mine was just one voice amongst many, as I allowed myself to be completely immersed in this

---

1 Port Navas is an area of outstanding peace and beauty in Cornwall. This is one of seven creeks of the Helford River ancestry which is approximately 7 miles west of Falmouth.

hymn, this chanting. It was much more than that – it was a primordial, elemental, animalistic exultant expression of being with it and in it and part of it. I arrived back at the bay exhilarated and drained all at the same time. I slept soundly and woke refreshed, ready to make my offering at the right moment, probably that day.

Most of the day passed, as the moment did not seem quite right, which really gave me time to contemplate all that had brought me here, and allow myself to be very present, in touch, very conscious of the moment. There came a time when there was a stillness all around me, the grey clouds were lifting and little bits of blue sky were visible. This seemed like the moment – there was a feeling of expectancy and of being watched.

I gathered up the sculpture in both arms and sat on the edge of the deck, leant out over the sea and prepared myself. I had a moment of feeling slightly stupid, and wondered what on earth I was doing, but it soon passed. I felt a sense of wonder and knew that this was an important moment. I remembered what David had said to me about this process, that in his experience it is really important to be aware of what happens afterwards. The moment after making the offering. So, as I lowered the head into the water with an old Palestinian scarf I had wrapped around its neck, I was wondering what would happen next. Would a flotilla of dolphins come charging past, would the skies open and reveal something wondrous, or would there be a great flash of lightning? All these things went through my head, with me expecting a great drama, the passing of the seas, or a plague of sea creatures.

The great, heavy brass sculpture of my head quietly went under the water, the scarf resisting for a brief moment, then following the head down into the depths. I felt that this should be the moment when I would achieve great clarity; maybe even God might be revealed to me, but something quite different happened. The sculpture very elegantly arose back to the surface of the water and quietly bobbed and nodded its way into the distance. At first, I was speechless, I couldn't quite believe my eyes, this was surely a miracle, but my brain had already started to understand the logic that there was probably an air pocket inside the casting giving the sculpture some flotation. The ordinariness of this explanation was a little disappointing but that was not what was going on inside my body. Deep, deep, down I felt a rumbling. I felt that the earth beneath me was shaking, but it was coming from within me. I opened my mouth to release the pressure and realised I was laughing. Great gulping, noisy earth-moving laughter shook me; I leant backwards and expelled this great noise of joy and laughter.

There might be many explanations or ways of interpreting this event: had Neptune rejected my offering? Was Aphrodite holding me up and showing me to the world? I don't know; but I do know I felt this great happiness, relief, sense of well-being, of being at peace. Ready for whatever would happen next, and that it certainly wasn't going to be what I expected. I had to be prepared for the unexpected – a message.

21

With Flying Colours

With flying colours: The colours are the national flag flown at sea during battle. A ship would surrender by lowering the colours and the term is now used to indicate a triumphant victory or win.

THE FINAL, IMPORTANT part of each Sailaday voyage would be coming home and it would be of great importance that we celebrated this returning. The important celebration of returning would start on the last evening of each voyage. We would reminisce and recount our successes, making sure that each person's part in the adventure was acknowledged. Taking pleasure in what we had achieved, however big or small, and trusting that they would be stored in our memories.

There would be time to review their initial contracts and to confirm whether they had achieved what they had set out to achieve. In some cases, this may not have happened, and space would be given to reassess the contract, talk about what changes they had made and how these were going to help them. I believe very strongly that people need to put into words what they have achieved. I felt it wasn't adequate for people just to say, *"I got what I wanted"*. I needed them to say, *"I got this..."*, *"I achieved that..."*, and *"This is how this experience is going to help me"*. Most participants would use the phrase, *"I got more than I ever expected..."*, and I would pursue this and check what they felt they had got out of it and why they had set their initial expectations so low.

Here is maybe a tip for those readers out there who go out and have their day golfing, walking or maybe sailing. At the end of the day, go home, sit down, have a drink, relax and review your day, before you turn on the television or carry on with the rest of your day. I can almost guarantee that you will be feeling different from when you set out earlier in the day. You can enhance this sensation by sharing it with somebody and speaking the words aloud, *"I feel...,"*

After our last formal group time, that evening we would come together over hot drinks and cake and sometimes people would sing or tell stories. We have been known to have music and dance – one notable occasion comes to mind when I was shown how to pole dance around the mast. There was always some grief around the ending, but these occasions were clearly happy, with a great deal of laughter which was always part of the Sailaday experience. Many times I have been told, *"I don't think I have ever laughed so much"*.

On the last day, before disembarkation, I would give each participant some personal feedback on their strengths, what their personal development learning edge might be, and how this experience might help them in the future.

I would also give each participant a small colourful picturesque object to take away, an attachment object[1], something that would help them maintain a link to their experience. This was a little concertina object with quotes and metaphors on each page:

"When breathing make more effort to exhale and to clean out the old, as in your recovery, make room for the new life and new energy."

"You know where you are starting from, before you can navigate to your goal."

"It had to get dark enough before you could see the stars."

"Your feelings won't harm you, but drugs and alcohol will."

"Recovery is change, it is letting go, it is a continuous process."

"It's the process that's important not necessarily the outcome."

"You can't change the weather, but you can trim your sails."

---

1   Attachment: Bowlby, J. (1969). *Attachment and Loss, volume 1: Attachment.* New York, NY: Basic Books. Attachment is primarily the seeking of proximity to an attachment figure, an adult who is sensitive and responsive, and can be a consistent caregiver. To maintain the attachment an object can be imbued with this power.

I would also give them a small gift on the very last morning. This would be a transitional object, something to take away with them and to hold onto and to touch and remind them of their experience.

If it was appropriate, and for most groups it would be, I would recount a story that many could identify with. A story about Japanese warriors.

"At the end of the Second World War, throughout the islands of the Pacific that had been invaded by the Japanese, there were still small groups and individual Japanese soldiers who had been left behind in the general retreat before the American onslaught. These warriors had dedicated their lives to fighting and were prepared to die for the Emperor; they had been holed up in caves and fortifications waiting to fight the Americans. Somehow, they were passed by, and most didn't even know the war had ended.

Sometimes, it would be many years later before these warriors gave up their positions and walked, or staggered, as they were in poor physical condition, down to the nearest habitation. Having bullied and terrorised the local population they were surprised, amazed and quite overwhelmed that they were made welcome, fed and clothed.

It could take quite some time for these men to be passed from island to island to get back to Japan. Here they were made welcome as great heroes and given the full honours of returning soldiers, for having held their posts and done most of what had been asked of them.

The veterans were treated with great respect and, although it wasn't an appropriate subject for celebration, they were hailed as important heroes. They were in a state of shock and trauma and found it very difficult to comprehend this turnabout in their fate. They saw themselves as failed soldiers and certainly found it hard to wear the mantle of hero warriors. They were full of shame. Slowly, little by little, most of them integrated and recovered. They all agreed that the hardest concept to bear and to understand was that their war was over."

At this point in the story, often there would be a communal intake of breath as the participants sensed the metaphor of the story. Their war was over, life would never be the same again, and they were brave and honoured people. When asked, they would often remark what a relief it was to be told this, and what joy to know they had survived and had their whole life ahead of them now. Many had come to understand, as had I, that they would never be the same again. The wind of change had come, and we were on a new course. There was nothing to be ashamed of in what they had done, and what they had had to do to survive.

Quite often I would be asked why I did this work. It had taken me a while to understand why, and to put into words. I know I felt blessed, having shared so intimately such a unique quest with people who were in a state of change and transition. I felt as though they were in a state of grace and I was privileged to be sharing it with them. I had a heightened awareness of the timelessness of treading where other healers had trodden many thousands of years ago. I was prepared to nurture and contain the vulnerable and damaged people who committed to journey with me, to take them in my hands and hold them while they met their demons. To bear witness to the discovery of a life renewed, strengthened and better founded to weather the journey ahead.

When I re-read these words, I am filled with gratitude and joy and I understand the process and the necessity of an ending. This book is part of that process of reminiscing and celebrating.

I will end with a poem from the C13th Sufi poet Rumi:

Silence

Silence lies in the ocean
While words flow through the river
The ocean waits for you
Don't wait for the river
Look to the ocean and watch its message
It will come, it will come.

References

Chapter 3

Eric Berne presented transactional analysis to the world as a phenomenological approach: Berne, E. (1961) *Transactional Analysis in Psychotherapy.* New York: Grove Press.

Berne E, (1957). *Ego States in Psychotherapy, American Journal of Psychotherapy,* 11(2), 293-309. Berne, E. (1976). *Classification of Positions,* Transactional Analysis Bulletin Selected Articles from Volumes 1 through 9. *Empathy And 'Empathism',* International Journal of Psychoanalysis, 78, 279-293.

Chapter 7

Developmental stages (Clarke & Dawson, 1998) of Being, Doing and Thinking which roughly correlate to Erikson EH, 1950, *Childhood and Society,* New York, Norton Erikson E, 1995, *Childhood and Society,* Paperback, New York, Vintage Erikson E, 1950, *Childhood and Society,* New York, Norton (Revised edn 1963)

Ilsley Clarke, J. and Dawson, C. (1998) *Growing Up Again: Parenting Ourselves Parenting Our Children.* Minnesota: Hazelden.

Chapter 13

Shapiro F, 1989, *Efficacy of the eye movement desensitisation procedure in the treatment of traumatic memories, Journal of Traumatic Stress*, 2, 199- 223

2012, *Getting Past Your Past: Take Control of Your Life with Self-Help Techniques from EMDR Therapy*, New York, Tudor K, 2003, *The neopsyche: the integrating adult ego state.*

Ego States (Key Concepts in Transactional Analysis), Worth Publishers

Chapter 17

Further reading on the negative impact of mindfulness

Kate Williams is a PhD researcher in psychology at the University of Manchester and a mindfulness teacher. She has said that "negative [mindful] experiences generally fall into one of two categories: a natural emotional response to self-exploration, which might be experienced as pleasant, unpleasant, or neutral; or the negative experiences can be quite extreme, to the extent of inducing paranoia, delusions, confusion, mania or depression." (Foster, 2016, para. 14–15).

Bessel Van der Kolk's experience had been that mindfulness doesn't work for traumatized people because they are not sufficiently connected to their emotions (Van der Kolk, 2011). Specifically, Van der Kolk sent numerous highly traumatized patients to do mindfulness exercises with John Kabat-Zinn, and he found that many of them were returning in a state of upset and agitation after those experiences. Van der Kolk explained that, as the patients became silent and started to pay attention to themselves during the meditation exercises, their internal sensations could be so intense that they felt overwhelmed and, without the tools to work through those sensations, they would dissociate.

Additional further reading

Foster, D. (2016, January). *Is mindfulness making us ill?* The Guardian. Retrieved from https://www.theguardian.com/lifeandstyle/2016/jan/23/is-mindfulness-making-us-ill

McDonagh, M. (2014, November). *The cult of mindfulness.* The Spectator. London, Australia. Available online at https://www.spectator.co.uk/article/the-cult-of-mindfulness-

Langone, M. (2019), *What counsellors should know about cult dynamics*, ICSA Today, 10(2), 6–7.

Chapter 19

Philip Cushman 1996 *Constructing the Self*; New York; Perseus

Taylor,Kuo & Sullivan; *Green play settings benefit children with ADD/ADHD*

Rose, et al; *Outdoor activity reduces myopia*

Lovasi, et al; *Children living on streets with trees have less asthma*

Preety et al; *Green exercise reduces blood pressure and improves mood*

Wells & Evans; *Nature buffers life stress amongst children*

Ulrich: *Views of nature improve recovery from surgery*

Poudayl, Hodges, Bowker, & Cordell,2009 *Life expectancy is related to presence of natural landscapes*

S. Levine, Poesis 1992 *The capacity to negotiate (and influence what is provided)*

St George and the Dragon is a legendary creature of folklore and mythology across central and eastern Europe, Bulgaria, Russia, Belarus, Ukraine, Serbia and Macedonia and most western European countries including the UK and Wales. The various versions of this story are told as a metaphor about good versus evil and is familiar to Christian theology, even though A this story is from a Muslim background. In the story, St George, who died in 303 A.D., saved the princess, stabbed the beast and subdued it, but my understanding of this story is that it is also a metaphor about addiction and co-dependancy.

Also see; Karpman SB, 1968, *Fairy tales and script drama analysis, Transactional Analysis, Bulletin*, 7.

Further reading

Lannowe Hall R & Parker Hall S 2008, *Addiction Today, Analysis of a marine wilderness therapeutic activity*

Lannowe Hall R & Parker Hall S, 2011, *International Stress Management* magazine. Analysis of the role of marine wilderness therapeutic activity in stress management.

Parker Hall S. 2008 *Anger rage and relationship; and an empathic approach to anger management*, London Routledge.

6IATC Presentation 2012

Ohlsson T, 2005, *TA therapy with drug addicts researched, Transactions*, No.3, ITA

Holmes J, 1998, *The British Journal of Medical Psychology, The changing aims of psychoanalytical psychotherapy, an integrative perspective*, 70,231/248

Ernst, F. (1971). *The OK Corral: The grid forget-on-with. Transactional Analysis Journal*, 1(4), pp. 33–42.

In Sills C & Hargaden H, *Key Concepts in Transactional Analysis, Ego States*, London, Worth Publishing

Winnicott DO, 1965, *The Maturational Processes and the Facilitating Environment*, London, Hogarth

Chamorro-Premuzic T ,2012, *Harvard Business Review*

Karpman SB, 1968, *Fairy tales and script drama analysis, Transactional Analysis*, Bulletin, 7.

Lieberman, M. D. et al.,2007, *Putting feelings into words: Affect labelling disrupts Amygdala activity in resposnse to affective stimuli, Psychological Science*, 18, 5: 421- 428.

Rennie DL, 1998, *Person-centred counselling: an experiential approach*, London, Sage

Holmes, J. (1998). *The British Journal of Medical Psychology, The changing aims of psychoanalytical psychotherapy, an integrative perspective*, 70, 231/248.

Affect Regulation and the Origin of Self, New Jersey, Laurence Erlbaum Associates

Tudor, K. (2003) *The Neopsyche: the integrating adult ego state*. In Sills, C. and Hargaden, H., *Key Concepts in Transactional Analysis: Ego States*. London: Worth Publishing.

Goulding, M. and Goulding, R. (1976) *Injunctions, decisions and redecisions. Transactional Analysis Journal*, 6, 1: 41–48.

Understanding sailing as a metaphor for living (recovery) 302 *Adventure*

Lightning Source UK Ltd.
Milton Keynes UK
UKHW021405060521
383165UK00008B/244